Mathematics in Nursery Education

Second Edition

Mathematics in Nursery Education

Second Edition

Ann Montague-Smith

 **David Fulton** Publishers

David Fulton Publishers Ltd
The Chiswick Centre, 414 Chiswick High Road, London W4 5TF

www.fultonpublishers.co.uk
www.onestopeducation.co.uk

First published in Great Britain in 1997 by David Fulton Publishers
Second edition published 2003, reprinted 2004, 2005

10 9 8 7 6 5 4

David Fulton Publishers is a division of Granada Learning Limited, part of ITV plc

British Library Cataloguing in Publication Data
A catalogue record for this book is available from the British Library.

ISBN 1 85346 866 5

Typeset by Textype Typesetters, Cambridge
Printed and bound in Great Britain

Contents

Introduction

With the introduction of the Foundation Stage Curriculum (DfEE, 2000) it seemed appropriate to prepare this second edition. Since writing the first edition a number of other books about early years mathematics have been published. However, I find my students still search for books which are detailed about the wealth of research evidence available, current good professional practice and appropriate mathematics concepts and content. I hope that this second edition will satisfy the need for why, what and how to teach mathematics for the Foundation Stage.

I have used the term 'nursery' to mean any pre-five educational setting, including nursery schools and classes, playgroups and day care. The term 'adult' refers to anyone who works within the setting. The book is intended for anyone who works with pre-fives children, teachers, nursery nurses, classroom assistants, playgroup leaders and workers, child-minders and day care staff. I hope that the reader finds it easy to read. There is a glossary of mathematical terms at the back for the specific mathematical vocabulary.

In each of Chapters 1 to 5 the book covers:

- the research evidence;
- the key concepts for the mathematical topics;
- how adults can help children to have appropriate mathematical experiences through planned and child-chosen activities;
- some examples of planned activities;
- suggestions for language development;
- help with assessment criteria.

An addition to the previous edition is the inclusion of 'key questions', matched to the learning objectives. These stem from the recently published 'Probing Questions', in *Assess and Review Lessons* produced by the National Numeracy Strategy team (2002) to help with assessment. The key questions have been trialled to some extent by PGCE students who found these very useful in identifying what the next steps in learning might be.

I chose to write about mathematics rather than concentrate solely upon the Foundation Stage Curriculum for mathematics, as the latter approach seemed to be more limiting in what could be considered within the book. The chapter headings of Counting, Number, Pattern, Shape and Space, and Measures were chosen as a means of identifying the mathematical content of the Foundation Stage Curriculum.

Counting is considered separately from Number because it is such an important aspect of understanding about mathematics with such a wealth of research evidence that it demands a chapter in its own right. Within each chapter there is a section on problem-solving within that mathematical topic. In Chapter 6 specific help with planning and assessment is given.

Two terms which are used throughout the book and which may need explaining are:

- *Circle time.* This is often used to bring all the children together for a story, or for singing songs. It can be used for a whole-group mathematical activity and examples of these are given within the book.
- *Focused activities.* These are planned activities with a stated purpose where the adult works with a group of children. There are examples of these in each chapter and suggestions for language development are included, as are suggestions for resources.

Finally, I hope that the second edition of this book fulfils its purpose, namely to encourage adults working with pre-fives to have increased understanding of the mathematics and to become more confident in planning, teaching and assessing mathematical learning.

Acknowledgements

My thanks to the staff and children of the first schools who allowed photographs of children at work to be taken, and for examples of work to be collected for inclusion in the book. To my PGCE students who trialled the concept maps and key questions my heart-felt thanks. To all those nurseries, playgroups and reception classes which I visited, both here in Britain and in Europe, my thanks for your enthusiastic support. To my friends whose children contributed drawings, my thanks for your patience. To my husband David, who took all the photographs for the book, listened to ideas and read the manuscript, making suggestions for improvements to this second edition: I could not have written this without all your help.

Ann Montague-Smith
University College Worcester
Email: a.montague-smith@worc.ac.uk
January 2002

CHAPTER 1
Counting

This is the first of two chapters about number. In this chapter the development of counting skills is considered in detail. Chapter 2, using counting skills, considers reading and recording numbers, numbers used in everyday life, and early number operations such as real-life addition and subtraction. The research reviewed in this chapter suggests that experience of counting, in different contexts, is the important aspect of learning to count effectively, and leads to developing understanding of numbers and number operations, such as addition and subtraction. Through this chapter it is intended to give an overview of the research findings, showing the counting skills which children may already have when they begin their nursery education, and showing ways in which understanding of number can be developed by taking note of the research findings about how children learn to count.

By the end of the reception stage in school, or for a four year old in a nursery class, the children are expected to be able to:

- Say and use number names in order in familiar contexts.
- Count reliably up to 10 everyday objects.
- Use developing mathematical ideas and methods to solve practical problems.

(DfEE, 2000)

There are Stepping Stones to show the developmental stages which children need in order to be able to meet the key objectives. The activity ideas within this chapter will help practitioners to develop children's understanding in the above aspects of counting.

1.1 Counting skills: from birth to four years

Babies

From just a few days old babies have the ability to recognise small groups of up to three objects (Macnamara, 1996). Baroody (1987) showed that infants as young as six months can distinguish the difference between groups of one and two, two and three, and three and four. The babies are shown pictures of three objects. At first the baby shows interest, but eventually this is lost. At this point a picture of two or four objects is shown and the baby shows interest again. Similarly, babies are exposed to a series of three sounds, and after a while their interest wanes until they hear two or four sounds. It is assumed that it is the 'threeness' which they no longer find interesting. Babies cannot distinguish between larger quantities, say four and five. There is no evidence that they understand that four is one more than three, merely that they perceive that there is a difference.

Toddlers

As toddlers, children are forming comparisons between the sizes of small groups of objects. Geist (2001) described how an 18-month old child dropped coloured balls over the side of a ball pit. He dropped one ball, then two more over the pit. Then he went to the other side of the pit and dropped two balls. He returned to the first side of the pit and looked again at the grouping of the three balls, then moved back to the second side and dropped another ball over the side. He now had two groups of three balls. He used visual perception rather than counting skills to form equal groups and showed an understanding of equality of quantity. At about two years of age children have begun to use the language of comparison, such as 'more', 'same' and 'different' (Wagner and Walters, 1982), to distinguish between quantities. Two year olds will 'count', using counting language, but not necessarily in counting order. Fuson *et al.* (1982) found that young children learn the difference between counting and non-counting words at a very early age and that by the age of two, some of them use counting words when asked to count collections of objects. Gelman and Gallistel (1986) carried out some counting experiments with two, three and four year olds which showed that two year olds can 'count' a row of objects, giving them counting names, one name for each object. These names may not be adult ones; some two year olds used number words, but in their own order, for example two, six, one, four, three. At this stage they have understood that to count, each item is given a number label.

Three year olds

The research of Beckmann and Descoeudres in the early 1920s (in Gelman and Gallistel, 1986) showed that three year olds can recognise small quantities of one, two and three consistently and accurately, but that for the larger quantities of four and five they were inconsistent and inaccurate, often representing four as three or five. They called this phenomenon 'un, deux, trois, beaucoup'. They found that the children saw quantities larger than three as undifferentiated 'lots'. Children's ability to recognise a small quantity and name how many has been called subitising. Children's ability to subitise for small quantities of one, two and three breaks down for amounts of four or five or more. There are two opposing views as to how children subitise. The Piagetian view is that children see small quantities of one, two and three as a pattern or arrangement and that they see each arrangement as a different arrangement that just happens to be labelled 'three' (Baroody, 1987) (Figure 1.1). In this view there is no understanding of number; it is just a label for an arrangement. Children are not expected to recognise that arrangements or patterns have both a wholeness which can be labelled with a number and individual elements until they reach the Piagetian stage of operational thinking.

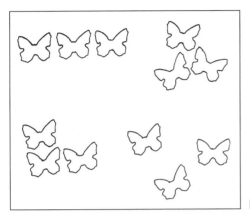

Figure 1.1 Different arrangements of three

Four year olds

At this age children develop the ability to make auditory–visual matches, such as linking the sound of three taps with three dots. As their verbal counting and object skills develop they are able to make comparisons of groups of objects larger than four (Baroody, 2000).

In a different view, counting precedes subitising. Children learn to count how many in small groups before they recognise the general set of 'three'. This view was put forward by Beckmann in the early 1920s (Baroody, 1987; Gelman and Gallistel, 1986). Through many experiences of counting, it is suggested that children begin to develop recognition of patterns of how many, that is, they see a pattern of 'threeness' which they respond to immediately.

It is quite possible that children can both recognise a number arrangement and count how many. This would depend upon the experiences of counting and recognising number arrangements that they have had, and on the size or the quantity. Where the quantity becomes larger, children would probably not recognise the arrangement and so counting skills would be needed.

Both models regard subitising as an essential skill in the child's developing understanding of number. Glaserfeld (Baroody, 1987) postulated that it is possible that from their ability to subitise, children may begin to form generalisations about number; for example, that sets that have the same number of objects do not need to be in the same arrangement.

It can be seen that by the time children begin nursery education, at three or four years of age, they may have already acquired some understanding of number. They may:

- recognise and name small quantities;
- appreciate that one group can have more than another or have the same quantity;

- know some number names, but not recite them in order;
- apply a number name tag to each item in order to count how many.

Experiences before children begin nursery education will be diverse, but most will have encountered counting through such activities as finger and toe counting games with parents, counting rhymes, and counting when shopping. However, the ability to count to four, five, six . . . does not mean that a child can count out that number of objects (Womack, 1988).

1.2 Theories about number development

There are two distinct views about how children develop the ability to understand and use number. The first of these, the Piagetian view, has affected thinking about how children are taught about number for at least the last thirty years. The second, the 'counting' view, is based on research from the 1970s and is gaining in acceptance as the way forward.

The Piagetian view

Here it is believed that children are incapable of understanding number until they are able to think logically, and to understand serial ordering, which, in Piaget's view, is essential in order to understand one-to-one correspondence relationships. To think logically, children need to be able to classify, that is, to sort objects into sets by a given criterion and to be able to answer questions about the set. For example, if there is a set of three toy cars and two toy lorries, can a child say whether there are more cars or more vehicles? (Figure 1.2).

Figure 1.2 Are there more horses or more animals?

Piaget (1965) found that children had difficulty with this type of question and so children were deemed not ready to understand number. However, subsequent research by Donaldson and others (Hughes, 1986) showed that where the question was embedded in a context which had meaning for children they had no difficulty in responding appropriately. For one-to-one correspondence, children need to be able to match each item in a group, first, second, third and so on, and to keep track of those they have already matched. Piaget believed that understanding number conservation was essential, that is, that whatever the arrangement of the objects to be counted, their quantity remained the same. Today, however, it is considered more important for young children to develop counting skills early in their lives, as discussed in detail below, and build upon these, to enable effective understanding about number to develop (Hughes, 1986).

The counting view

In this view, it is believed that the experience of counting develops understanding of number, and that this understanding evolves gradually through the counting experiences. Children may begin by using counting words mechanically, first repeating them without any meaning attached, and then beginning to count objects, gradually moving to a more sophisticated view of counting and its relationship to number. In this view, the development of counting skills runs alongside the development of number concepts and these are inextricably entwined (Baroody, 1987; Gelman and Gallistel, 1986; Thompson, 1995).

How teachers teach

It is from the Piagetian theory that the sorting, matching and ordering of sets of objects, as a precursor to understanding number, has grown (Gardner *et al.*, 1973) and this has been reflected in the traditional view of nursery and reception teaching. This view has been questioned by Gelman (1972 a,b), Fuson *et al.* (1982) and Thompson (1995) who believe that the evidence points to the experience of counting as the important key to children's developing understanding about number. It is this second view that is adopted in this book; that is, that sorting and matching experiences do not lead by themselves to an understanding of number. However, the importance of classification is acknowledged, both as a context for counting and as essential for developing skills and understanding in handling data.

1.3 Developing counting skills in the nursery

From the mass of evidence of how children learn to count, Gelman and Gallistel (1986) produced five principles which state the counting concepts which children need to acquire to become proficient at counting. These are:

- the one–one principle;
- the stable-order principle;
- the cardinal principle;
- the abstraction principle;
- the order-irrelevance principle.

The one–one principle

This is the matching of counting words to the items to be counted. Children need to understand that each number word can only be used once and that every item in the set must be assigned a number word, or tagged. To do this effectively, the number words need to be used in order and the items to be counted partitioned into two sets, a set of items which have already been tagged and those to be tagged.

To understand the one–one principle children will need to:

- Learn to recite the counting words in order. As has been seen in Section 1.1, children as young as two years old, can 'count', although they may not use the number words in proper order.
- Touch and count each item only once. Children will find it helpful to partition the items as they count, that is, to touch and move the items one by one into a counted pile. This will help them to be aware of which items have been counted. Research has shown that young children find it easier to touch and count where the objects are placed in a straight line, rather than in a random arrangement (Potter and Levy, 1968). Where objects are placed in a circle arrangement, children may forget where they started their count and so count on again. For the early stages of counting, the partitioning of the set into counted and not counted is an important factor in accuracy of counting.
- Coordinate the touch and count so that these happen at the same time. Young children, when asked to count some items, will point to the items as they count. This seems to be an important aspect of the early counting process, as it probably helps to ensure that each item is considered and touched simultaneously and just once (Gelman and Gallistel, 1986).

There are some common errors that children often make when using the one–one principle. These are:

- touching an item to be counted more than once, so that it is counted again;
- missing an item altogether;
- repeating the counting name or tag;
- missing out counting names or tags;
- failing to coordinate the touch and count.

The stable-order principle

As well as assigning a counting word to each item in the set to be counted, children must learn to repeat the counting words in order. Counting words in the English language have no recognisable pattern to them until fourteen, fifteen, sixteen . . . Learning to count involves rote learning of the counting names and from one to thirteen there is no discernible pattern in English and these words will be learnt, in order, by rote. The pattern within each decade is recognisable, that is, twenty-one, twenty-two . . . and then each new decade name, thirty, forty, must be learnt. As children become proficient counters to ten, then twenty, they sometimes continue to count without recognising the decade change as the following example of Liam's counting (5 years 5 months) shows:

> one, two, three . . . eighteen, nineteen, twenty, twenty-one . . . twenty-nine, twenty-ten, twenty-eleven, twenty-twelve . . . twenty-twenty.

At first children will 'chant' numbers, perhaps learnt through number rhymes and stories, and this chant will appear to have no meaning. Gradually, the order of the words takes on meaning and becomes related to items to be counted. Children begin to realise that the order of the counting words is always the same and that in order to count they must reproduce this order. This is the stable-order principle.

The cardinal principle

The final number in the count, that is the cardinal number of the set, represents how many are in the set. In order to say how many in a set, children need to recognise that the last number in their count represents how many there are in the set, so that as well as touching and counting one–one, using the counting names in order and consistently, they must be able to stop on the last number of the count and recognise that as how many there are. The cardinal principle is dependent upon the one–one and the stable-order principles and is a later stage of development.

These first three principles are called the 'how to count' principles (Gelman and Gallistel, 1986). Bird (1991) defines four coordination skills in counting:

- using a counting word for each object;
- counting each object just once;
- stopping the count at the correct point;
- using the counting words in the correct order, starting and stopping at the right place.

To this should be added:

- understanding that the last number in the count represents the cardinal number of the set.

The abstraction principle

This principle states that the how-to-count procedure can be applied to any counting situation. Children can count any set, whether it is made up of similar objects (such as toy cars) or unlike objects (such as a doll, ball, plate and shoe). In counting a set of similar objects a child might say 'There are four cars'. Here the child is able to name the set as cars. However, where the objects are unlike they will need to find a common property of the set, such as 'There are four things'. Adults know that anything can be counted, whether it can be seen or imagined, and anything can be grouped together to be counted. Gast (1957, in Gelman and Gallistel, 1986) suggests that three and four year olds can only count things which are identical with each other and that any variation in the material, by colour for example, causes a break in the ability to count. This argument has fed the notion that pre-number activities must be based upon sorting and classifying activities. However, it is now thought that practical experience of counting is what determines the child's development and so children should be encouraged to count any set which they have compiled, and which they see as countable.

The order-irrelevance principle

Given a set of a toy car, lorry, motorbike, bus and fire engine, arranged in a line, adults know that it is quite acceptable to call the car 'one' on the first count and the lorry 'one' on the second. In other words, the order in which items are counted does not affect the cardinal number of the set. Young children will not have this understanding and will need experience of counting the sets in different orders to begin to appreciate that the order of counting does not affect the cardinal number of the set. Once this fact has been understood children are said to know the following (Gelman and Gallistel, 1986):

- something counted is a thing, not a one or a two;
- the counting numbers are used as counting tags for the objects to be counted, and once the count is over, they no longer belong to those objects;
- in whatever order the objects are counted, the cardinal number of the set remains the same.

There is evidence from Carraher and Schliemann (1990) that many young children's counting experience is limited to using counting objects, such as cubes, or logic blocks. They suggest that this can affect the formation of place-value concepts at a later stage, and that children should have other counting experiences, including using coins, where from the start they will give the coin a tag which includes a number name, two pence, five pence and so on. If this suggestion is followed, then children will experience, from an early age, number words being used as a naming label for an object, which also describe their 'worth'. However, in their research Carraher and Schliemann found that most five year olds counted money, whatever the value of the coin, as 'ones'. Most nursery settings have a shop or café, and the role play of counting out money and using money names does seem to be of more importance at this stage than encouraging children to make abstract connections between the value of the coin and the count.

1.4 Concepts and skills associated with counting

The theoretical aspects of how children learn to count and develop understanding of number need to inform the way in which children are taught about number. Aubrey (1993) found that children entering reception classes had already, in most cases, developed the ability to understand and use counting and to use methods of recording. These findings can be related to the nursery school, where, following reflection upon the research evidence reported above, teachers will probably find that many children entering nursery provision will already have begun to develop skills in counting and thus the challenge is for nursery staff to provide counting experiences which take account of the child's current stage of development. In this section, a conceptual development for counting and understanding about number is discussed, one which can form the basis of planning in the nursery.

Equivalence

Equivalence refers to two sets which contain different items but have the sameness of quantity. For example, a tray with five farm animals has the number equivalence of a tray with five toy cars. Through learning to count children will begin to identify the numerical equivalence of sets, which is an abstraction of the number property from the counting situation. It is believed that children probably learn about equivalence through counting small sets of one to four items and through observing that these match up numerically (Baroody, 1987). Some items will come in pairs: eyes, ears, legs, arms . . . and these are referred to as 'two'. From this and similar experiences children abstract 'two' as being a label which can apply in any situation, with any set, where the number of objects is two.

Gelman and Gallistel (1986) found that children's recognition of equivalence depended upon their counting skills, that is, in order to recognise the equivalence of two sets, they counted both sets. If their cardinal values were the same then the sets were equivalent, if not then they were not equivalent.

Counting development

Steffe and Cobb (1998, cited in Pepper and Hunting, 1998) suggested that children move from the need to use concrete materials to count, such as counting all of the blocks on the table, to the ability to count using the numbers abstractly, such as counting on from a number without the need to say the preceding numbers, such as saying 'eight, nine, ten . . .' They categorised counting competency levels as follows:

1. *Counting using perceptual unit items:* using materials for counting, and to solve simple addition problems. Without the materials, such as counters or blocks, the children cannot carry out the activity.
2. *Counting using pictorial representations:* so in a simple task where some of the items to be added together are hidden, the child draws these in or makes tallies to represent them, then counts.
3. *Counting using a motor action:* the child makes, for example, a hand movement, pointing, or putting up fingers, to represent an amount that has been hidden.
4. *Counting aloud:* saying the number names as the child counts and internalising the motor action. The child does not need to touch the items.
5. *Counting abstract items:* this is shown where a child is able to count on from a given number, such as in 5+3, the child would say *five; six, seven, eight* and would know that eight represented the total.

Key experiences

From the five principles of success in counting, there are key experiences which children need in order to become successful at counting. These are opportunities to:

- use language of quantity to make comparisons, such as more, the same;
- recite the number names in order to become consistent;
- count items in a set:
  - which can be partitioned (moved)
  - count the same set again, with the items in a different order/array
  - count items which can be touched but not moved (items in a picture)
  - count items which can be seen but not touched
  - count sounds
  - count physical movements
- count out a given quantity of items.

This is a long list, but each experience will relate to a range of activities which are part of the normal curriculum of the nursery. To develop proficiency in counting, it is not enough just to develop the ability to count objects which can be touched. Using small quantities, children will develop eye coordination with counting in order to count objects which they can see but not touch, perhaps by ordering their counting according to the placing of the objects. Similarly with hearing and counting they will begin to understand that anything can be counted, not just items that can be seen and touched.

Use language of quantity to make comparisons

It may not be clear to the observer whether children subitise or count when comparing small quantities, such as for 'more', or 'the same'. Through these experiences they will begin to develop their understanding of equivalence and non-equivalence, and develop the associated language. Comparative language can be developed whilst making comparisons between sets, such as, when they are playing with the farm pieces, encouraging children to understand and use language such as lots, few, too many. When children are working with miniworlds an adult can take opportunities to extend the children's understanding of number language:

Please put lots of sheep in this field.
Will you put a few cows with the sheep?
Are there more cows or more sheep?
How do you know?

Shall we put more chairs into the doll's house kitchen?
Will you help me to put the dolls on the chairs?
Are there enough chairs for all the dolls? How can we tell?
How many chairs are there? Will you count them for me?

I wonder which cars need some petrol?
Shall we line them up by the petrol pump?
Lots of cars need petrol!
How many are there in this line?
I'll put the other cars in the parking spaces.
Are there more cars here (points to petrol pump) or here (points to parking spaces)?

Listening to children's conversations may give evidence of more developed counting skills than were realised. Sara, two years six months, and Jake, three years two months, were playing with buttons and had hidden some in their tightly closed hands. The following was overheard by an adult:

Jake: You've got more than me.
Sara: More.
Jake: Yes. I've got three and you've got two. I've got one more.

Comparisons such as 'few', 'not many' and 'lots' or 'more' can be made and understood at this stage. 'Fewer' can be used when comparing quantities: 'There are fewer plates than cups on the table.' This is less commonly used; we are more likely to say 'There are more cups than plates on the table.' Language such as 'a few more' and 'a lot less' can be very confusing to young children because of the qualifiers 'few' with 'more' and 'a lot' with 'less'. Where such language is used, care must be taken to ensure that the children understand what is meant within the context of the experience.

Consistently recite the number names in order

Some children will already be able to recite the number names to ten or more by the time they are three years old. Others will be just beginning to do this. Singing action number songs and rhymes, stories which involve counting, taking opportunities in the nursery to count, such as counting how many children are sitting at the table at snack time, or how many candles are on the birthday cake, will enable children to hear the counting names in order, and to begin to recognise that these form an order which is always the same. At the same time as learning to recite the counting names, these can be applied to counting, so for example a child who is still unfamiliar with the order of counting names can count, with help, how many people are working in the sand tray.

Rhythmic counting helps children to focus upon the word pattern of the counting numbers. This can be experienced through action number rhymes and songs, and can also be a game, where children clap or wave their arms in time to the count.

Count items in a set

To become competent at counting objects, children benefit from having a wide range of counting experiences. Consistent counting of items shows that children are developing the principles of counting. In order to help them to realise that anything can be counted the following experiences are helpful:

- *Count items which can be partitioned:* children move items to one side as they are counted.
- *Count the same set again, with the items in a different order/array:* here the items can be arranged in a straight line; a circle; an array. Each time the child points and touches and can move them if they wish. Gradually they should become aware that the cardinal number of the set remains constant.

- *Count items which can be touched but not moved (items in a picture):* here the children will need to consider how to group the objects visually so that they are sure that they count each one just once.
- *Count items which can be seen but not touched:* this is more difficult and relies upon visual grouping clues to remind the child what has already been counted.
- *Count sounds:* children listen, perhaps with their eyes shut, to sounds and count them. This will help them to realise that items to be counted do not have to be things that can be seen or touched and eventually they will accept that anything that can be defined by humans can be counted, including things they imagine.
- *Count physical movements.* This helps children to 'feel' the counting, linking movement with the count. This can include activities such as making three hops, and playing games where pieces are moved on a game board. Hughes (1986) found that some nursery-aged children counted the square on which their counter started as 'one' so that they lost one square for each turn. He also found that where they needed to pass another counter on the board, they jumped over that square, without counting it. These are likely to be issues to be discussed with children as they play board games.
- *Count out a given quantity of items.* This involves understanding the spoken quantity and matching that with the final number in the count. Incidental experiences of this will occur regularly through the day, such as 'Please put four biscuits on the plate'; 'Please find three pencils'.

Whilst opportunities for counting will arise spontaneously from the children's work in the nursery, some opportunities may be planned, through games and group activities, so that all children experience the opportunities to count listed above, in a variety of contexts. Their ability to count may not include understanding of all the five principles in Section 1.3 above by the time they move into the reception class, or Year 1, but it is likely that they will be becoming proficient in counting in a range of situations and be beginning to understand how to count (abstraction principle) even if the order-irrelevance principle is not fully understood yet.

Concept map (Table 1.1)

This shows the concepts outlined above in matrix form, together with examples of vocabulary which can be developed. Some example activities are included to demonstrate how these concepts might be explored in a nursery setting. The map can be used as a basis for planning (and see Section 1.5 below). Some assessment checkpoints and key questions are given to show possible learning outcomes from the activities (and see Section 1.6 below).

1.5 Planning counting experiences

The range of counting experiences needed to develop understanding of number will come from both planned activities and incidental interventions from adults in children's play. Counting can occur in any nursery play environment and it is the

Table 1.1 Concept map for counting

Key concept	Vocabulary	Examples of activities	Assessment checkpoints	Key questions
Use language of quantity to make comparisons, such as more, the same	More, the same, less, fewer, different, enough, not enough, too many, nearly the same . . . , count Counting numbers: zero, one, two, three . . .	Comparing quantities of items in miniworlds; in block play; putting out and tidying away; lacing beads; counting out fruit or biscuits at snack time	• Responds appropriately to vocabulary • Uses vocabulary in context	• Have we enough? • How can you be sure that you have counted all of them? • Who has more/fewer? • What if I have one more/fewer, now who has more/fewer?
Consistently recite the number names in order	Counting numbers one to ten and beyond	Action number rhymes; number stories; counting out biscuits for snack time; rhythmic counting	• Recites the number names in order to five, ten, beyond ten to . . .	• Why do we have to say the number names in the same order when we count? • What would happen if we didn't start with one? • How can you be sure that you have said all of the number names?
Count items which can be partitioned (moved)	Counting numbers	Counting: some farm animals; beads on a lace; pennies in a purse	• Counts each item only once • Coordinates the count with the partition	• How many did you count? • How many . . . are there? • How many have you counted now? How many are there still to count? How do you know that?
Count the same set again, with the items in a different order/array	Counting numbers; in a line; in a circle; make a new group	Counting some buttons; rearranging them and counting them again; and again	• Counts each item only once • Starts with a different item as 'one' • Counts same items in different arrays	• How many have you counted? • What if you started with . . . are there the same number? How do you know that? • What if you put them in a different group; how many now? How do you know?

Table 1.1 (continued)

Count items which can be touched but not moved (e.g. items in a picture)	Counting numbers	Counting spots on dice; pictures on a page; spots children have stuck onto a collage	• Counts each item • Counts each item only once	• How many are there? • How do you know you have counted them all?
Count items which can be seen but not touched	Counting numbers	Counting pictures on a wall frieze; trees in a field; chimneys on a house	• Counts each item • Counts each item only once	• How many are there? • How do you know you have counted them all?
Count sounds	Counting numbers	Counting hand claps; taps on a drum; chiming of a clock	• Counts each sound • Counts each sound only once	• How many are there? • What if I tapped once more; how many then?

Count physical movements	Counting numbers	Counting hops, skips, throws of a ball; counting on a game board such as ludo, snakes and ladders	• Coordinates movement with the count
			• Counts each move
			• Counts each move only once
				• How many did you count?
				• (On a game board)
				  Where did you start?
				  How many did you count?
				  Where did you land?

Count out a given quantity of items	Counting numbers	Counting biscuits for snack time; pencils for drawing	• Counts out required number of items	• How many do you need? • How many did you count? • What if you need one more/fewer; how many then?
Use developing mathematical ideas and methods to solve practical problems	What could we try next? How did you work it out? Count, sort, group, set, match, list	Are there enough?: matching the count of two sets of objects	• Uses counting strategies to solve problems	• How many do you need? • How do you know that? • How did you work it out? • What could we try next?

skill of the adult to engage with the children and to help them to extend their language of number and their understanding through careful, sensitive questioning.

Setting up environments

Counting materials

Provide materials which can be counted. These can be specific collections of interesting items and trays with mixed collections, or items placed in an environment with the specific purpose of encouraging counting, such as shells and pebbles in the sand tray; carrots and potatoes in the kitchen area; coins and purses in the shop; skittles and balls as part of outdoor play. These items should be available for the children to choose on free access as well as usual items such as beads and laces, farm and animals, garage and cars, and so on.

Books, rhymes and songs

In the book area, encourage counting by ensuring that the books with pictures that encourage counting are placed on easy access, perhaps as part of a special display. These can be used during circle time, with all the children, or as part of a focused activity with a small group of children. Counting rhymes and songs, particularly those with actions, help children to recite the number names in order. Some number rhymes count up in ones, such as 'One, two, three, four, five, Once I caught a fish alive', 'One, two, buckle my shoe', and 'Peter taps with one hammer'. Some rhymes count down, for example 'Five currant buns in the baker's shop', 'Ten in the bed' and 'Ten green bottles'. All of these help children to recognise the counting patterns and to remember the order of the counting names. There are many good quality books and audiotapes of nursery rhymes and songs which include counting rhymes.

Number frieze

A number frieze in the nursery shows the link between the numeral and its cardinal value, for example, 3 and a picture of three frogs. Similarly, where children place their name cards on a board to show where they are working, there will be a limit to how many can work there (Figure 1.3). They will learn to recognise how many, and check to see if there is a space for them. A number line, where the numerals can be placed in order, is a most worthwhile resource. The numerals can be large, perhaps half the height of the children themselves. If the numerals are made from tactile materials, then the children can also experience touching and tracing the shapes of the numerals. Such a number line can become part of the children's play, where they decide how they will use it. Carruthers (1997) describes how the children developed games which involved the numerals, made personal choices of numerals, such as their age numerals, and made their own, written number lines.

Counting display

An interactive number display can be set up, on a table or cupboard top, which children use to explore counting. This might include a numeral for the day, say 4,

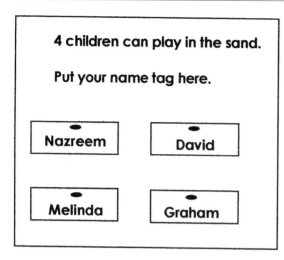

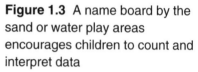

Figure 1.3 A name board by the sand or water play areas encourages children to count and interpret data

with pegs and pegboards, beads and laces, small cubes. Children count out four pegs and make a pattern on the pegboard with them. They can see how many different patterns of four they can make.

Number games

Number games, such as simple dice and board games, number dominoes and number snap games, can be available as games for the children to choose during their work time or as part of a focused activity with an adult. They should all become familiar with counting games using a dice and board, and number-matching games with playing cards, lotto and dominoes. Games which require children to throw a 'six' or another 'magic' number before they start to play can be counter-productive at this age, as children want to play the game, not wait for a dice start number.

Ben, Laura and Gary were four years and eight months old. Laura and Gary had both thrown sixes and had had two goes each.

Ben: When can I have a go? (Throws again; still not a six.)
Laura: Look, I've got another six. I've nearly won.
Gary: A four!
Ben: It's not fair. I still can't start. Just a two.
Laura: I've won!

And Ben burst into tears. The game had been won and he hadn't started because he did not throw a six.

Adult intervention in children's play

The skill of the adult worker in the nursery is in recognising when it is appropriate to intervene in children's play. The intervention needs to extend the children's understanding, through careful discussion and questioning, encouraging children to use the counting language that they have developed so far, and helping them to become familiar with new vocabulary. Insisting that children count when they are happily engaged in purposeful play is unlikely to develop positive attitudes to counting. Instead, the intervention must be supportive of what children are doing. The following are everyday examples of events in the nursery:

- Jack has been watching the swifts flying around the school roof. An adult asks him about the swifts. Jack says there are so many! The adult suggests that they see how many they can count together.
- Mai Ling has made a picture of a flower using magnetic tiles. She has given the flower two leaves. The adult asks her if the flower should have more leaves. Mai Ling says no; two is enough.
- Tim and Anna decide to build a slide for the dumper trucks with the large blocks. They ask an adult to help them carry the pieces outside. The adult asks how many they think they will need. Tim says three; Anna says more than that! So they agree to count as they carry them out to see how many they do need.
- Susie is sitting quietly, counting out dough cakes for teddy. One, two, five, three. The adult asks how many cakes teddy has. Susie says 'Lots!' They count them together.

All adults in the nursery should be aware of the need to intervene with sensitivity in the children's play, taking account of what the children are doing and why. Listening to the children will help the adult to take note of children's purpose in their play. All adults working in the nursery on that day should be aware of what has been planned, both in setting up environments and in focus tasks which an adult leads, and why, and the types of questions which would help to extend the children's thinking. Where the planning is specific, with clearly identified learning experiences identified, and with possibilities for language development specified, then all adults will be more aware of opportunities to make purposeful, successful interventions in children's play.

Developing problem-solving strategies through counting

Counting in itself is a problem-solving strategy, which can be used to answer questions. These questions will lead on to more challenging ones, such as how many more? Children's ability to count is an essential part of their growing understanding of number and they should be encouraged to ask themselves, and be asked, questions such as the following in meaningful contexts:

- *How many?* Ghopal wanted to nail two pieces of wood together. He asked Mark to pass him some nails. 'How many do you need?' asked Mark.
- *Who has more?* Joanna was working in the outdoor sandpit making sand pies and decorating them with flags. She had made four sand pies. She counted them. Then she counted the flags as she put them onto the sand pies. 'One, two, three, four. That's just right. There's one for each!'
- *Are there enough?* Steven was assisting a parent helper to put out the biscuits for his group for snack time. He said, as he put out the biscuits on a plate, 'Jo is here and

Maria and Lisa. That's one, two, three. That's three biscuits.' The parent reminded him that there were four in the group. 'Four. Oh silly me. I forgot me! That's one, two, three, four. Four biscuits!'

- *Is there the same number in each?* The nursery nurse took a small group of children into the nursery garden to look at ladybirds. They collected some and put them into specimen pots. Gavin said 'This ladybird has six spots.' They decided to check each ladybird they collected to see if they all had the same number of spots.

Focused activities

A focused activity is one that is planned with specific learning experiences and outcomes in mind, to be taught by an adult. In a nursery which uses the High Scope organisation, this would be Small Group Time. In another setting this could be the time when an adult withdraws a small group of children for a specific activity, or when a small group are encouraged to join an adult in, for example, the café, where they role-play serving, ordering, and giving and receiving money. Carefully planned focused activities for developing counting skills will ensure that over a period of time children experience activities designed to develop the key concepts as outlined in Section 1.4 above.

Where the key concepts are identified through a range of activities planned over a period of time, all children should receive a wide experience of counting in a range of different contexts and for different purposes. The following three examples of planned counting activities show the underlying thinking behind the planning. It is worth noting that the planning includes the concepts to be developed and the learning outcomes which might be observed. These elements of the planning help to ensure that the purpose of these activities is clear to the adults. It is suggested that the purpose of the activity be made clear to the children at the beginning of the session. The third example shows how counting skills can be developed through a topic approach.

Farm animals

An activity for a group of up to six children:

- *Purpose:*   to count out given quantities, matching the numeral to the count; to compare quantities and use appropriate number language.
- *Materials:*   sets of farm animals and farm buildings and fields.
- *Language:*   number words, number, count, more, the same, nearly the same, match . . .

How to begin

Put the animals on the table and ask the children to sort them into groups. Discuss their sortings and why they have chosen these groupings.

Ask the children to choose a group. Some questions that can be asked:

- How many animals are there in your set?
- Which group has more than yours?
- Which group has the same number as yours?

Ask the children to take turns to count out a given quantity. Let the others watch and check, which will give them experience of counting without touching:

- Beth, please put three sheep in the field.
- Let's count them together: one, two, three. Yes, three sheep.
- Now, Kerry, will you put four cows in the cowshed?
- David, how many sheepdogs shall we put with the sheep?

Children can ask each other questions using numbers and number language, and try new vocabulary.

Number rhymes and stories

An activity for everyone as part of circle time, or for a small group:

- *Purpose:* to learn the order of the counting numbers;
  to begin to recognise that the order of the counting numbers is stable.
- *Materials:* a selection of counting rhymes where the count is ordered forward from one. Puppets or dressing up clothes can be used if the rhymes are to be acted. A story which uses number, for example *When I Was One* by Colin and Jacqui Hawkins (Picture Puffin).
- *Language:* counting number words.

How to begin

Choose a favourite counting rhyme where the counting goes forward, such as 'Peter taps with one hammer'. Children sing this, copying the actions in time with the song.

Sing or recite other rhymes where the counting goes forwards, such as 'One, two, buckle my shoe'; 'One, two, three, mother caught a flea'; 'One, two, three, four, Mary at the cottage door'.

Rhythmic counting

Encourage the children to repeat a sequence of numbers with you, alternately slapping knees and clapping hands to make a rhythm at the same time:

Say:	one	two	one	two	one	two	one	two	one	two . . .
Action:	slap	clap	slap	clap	slap	clap	slap	clap	slap	clap . . .

Say:	one	two	three	four	one	two	three	four	one	two . . .
Action:	slap	clap	slap	clap	slap	clap	slap	clap	slap	clap . . .

Count in threes, slapping knees, clapping hands, hands on heads:

Say:	one	two	three	one	two	three	one	two	three	one . . .
Action:	slap	clap	head	slap	clap	head	slap	clap	head	slap . . .

Count in fives, this time saying the numbers one to four quietly, and five loudly:

Say:	one	two	three	four	five	one	two	three	four	five . . .
Action:	quiet	quiet	quiet	quiet	loud	quiet	quiet	quiet	quiet	loud . . .

A number story

Read a number story. *When I Was One* by Colin and Jacqui Hawkins (Picture Puffin) counts each birthday. Ask:

- Who has a birthday this week? How old will you be? Let's count to four . . .
- Who is nearly five years old? Let's count to five . . .
- Who has a brother or sister who is more than five? . . . Let's count to . . .

Topic: Growing

Planting seeds

An activity for everyone, to be completed through the week in small groups of about four:

- *Purpose:*   to count out a given quantity.
- *Materials:*   newspapers; bean seeds; compost; washing-up bowl or bucket; water in a jug; a plant pot for each child; label with child's name on it; felt-tipped pens.
- *Language:*   counting words, how many, more, the same, nearly . . .

How to begin

Ask the children to put newspaper on the table. Discuss growing plants, and give each child some bean seeds to examine. Put the compost in the bowl and help the children to pour water in until it is damp enough to be used. Each child fills their plant pot with compost and then they count out some beans.

- How many beans shall we plant in each pot?
- Count out two seeds for your pot. Will that be enough?
- Will three seeds fit in your pot? What about four?

When the number of seeds has been agreed, children can write how many seeds they have planted on their plant label, using their own marks, tallies, or, if they are able, writing a numeral. (See Chapter 2 for discussion on writing numerals.) Each child sticks their label to their plant pot.

On a daily basis, children check their pots, water them when necessary, and watch for growth. They read how many they have planted from their label and, over time, can check how many of their seeds grow. When the plants are large enough, they can be planted out in the nursery garden, or taken home to be planted out in the garden or in a grow bag.

Involving adult helpers in the planned activities

Where there are children whose home language is not English, there will be opportunities for helpers to encourage these children to count in their home language as well as in English. Parents may be encouraged in to help with this, and there may be adult workers in the nursery who speak the home language.

When the nursery staff meet together to plan, they can check that they are aware of the range of counting activities available during the sessions and agree on the vocabulary which they will try to encourage during that day or week. Where other adults have not been involved at the planning stage, perhaps because they are voluntary helpers, it is very helpful for them to have a prompt sheet (Table 1.2) which lists briefly the planned activities and their purpose, and gives a few examples of questions which can be used to encourage the children to use their growing understanding of number.

Counting activities for nursery environments

Table 1.3 shows suggestions for the range of opportunities for counting which can be planned, either through placing materials in an environment and encouraging children in their use of them to explore the language and actions of counting, or by using these suggestions as a basis for planned, focused activities.

Table 1.2 Example of a daily planning sheet for all the adults in the nursery

Tuesday morning:	
9.00am	Welcome children into the nursery. Jill: book area. Zena: table top area: patterns of five using magnetic tiles; how many? how many more? show me more than five. Mary: craft table: making a pattern using five things each time; circle patterns; straight line; other arrangements; make one with more than five. June: outside. Margaret (parent helper): please would you choose three or four children to help to prepare snacks and drinks. Five pieces of fruit on each plate: are there enough? do these have the same?
9.40	Clearing up.
9.50	Into main hall for movement session.
10.10	Into groups. Registers. Snack time: counting out in fives (five pieces of fruit on each plate).
10.30	Focus activity for Jill's and Zena's groups in Rainbow Room: counting five objects and pictures. Margaret: table top area: dice games. Mary: outside: feeding the pets. June: outside: by the climbing equipment.
11.10	Clearing up. Jill: Circle time. Number rhymes with 'five'. Story: Peepo by Janet and Allan Ahlberg (Picture Puffin).

Table 1.3 Counting activities for nursery environments

Environment	Concept/skill	Context
circle time	• stable order counting • count how many • show a given number, e.g. of fingers	• counting stories • number action rhymes • acting out a story: dressing up; using puppets
daily routines	• count how many • count out a given quantity	• taking the register • counting the group • counting out snacks, drinks • counting out/away, e.g. paint-brushes, scissors • counting how many can work in the sand, water . . .
art and craft areas	• count by touching and partitioning • count pictures • compare quantities	• counting how many, to make a collage: pieces of scrap paper, pasta shells, shiny things . . . • sticking pictures cut from a catalogue: counting how many . . . • painting a picture: counting how many . . . • making dough models: counting how many models, two eyes, four legs . . . ; which has more legs . . .
table top games and collections	• count by touching and partitioning • use subitising skills to recognise how many • count physical movements	• counting how many: beads on a lace; pegs on a peg board . . . • recognising quantities: playing number snap, lotto . . . • counting along a track: board games with dice
sand and water	• count out a given quantity • count how many • compare quantities	• making three, four, sand pies • putting four cups of water in the water wheel • are there enough flags for one for each sand pie? • are there enough captains for one for each boat?
construction	• counting out a given quantity • count how many • compare quantities • making two groups the same	• making a tower with five bricks • counting how many big blocks to make a road • comparing two towers: which has more? • this tower has more; make that one have the same number of bricks
role play	• counting out a given quantity • count how many • compare quantities	• dressing up: role playing, e.g. The Three Bears: chairs, beds, porridge • shopping, playing customer/shopkeeper roles: counting out coins • preparing food in the home area: counting out enough plates for the four guests
miniworlds	• counting out a given quantity • count how many • compare quantities	• doll's house: putting three people in the kitchen; two in the bedroom . . . • road floor plan: counting how many cars on this road; how many lorries . . . • are there enough people to fill the seats in this car? • are there enough chairs for all the people in the doll's house?
outside play	• counting how many • comparing quantities	• playing skittles: how many did you knock down? • who can collect more conkers than this? • sequences: two steps, one jump . . . • counting three balls to put in the truck to take over there . . .

1.6 Assessment

What to look for

Regular observations of individual children, noting their use of language and how they count, will give useful evidence of what children can do and what they understand, and identify aspects of counting where children lack confidence. Use the assessment checkpoints and key questions in Table 1.1 to help with assessment. The questions include both closed (how many?) and open (how do you know?) types. Observations, with evidence of the child's behaviour to support their understanding, can be recorded. Where evidence of achievement in a standard form is required, the observational evidence can be supported by a note of the assessment checkpoint, with date and comment attached to show when the evidence of achievement was noted. Regular observations will show whether a child:

- Knows number names in order to . . .
- Knows that the last number in the count is the cardinal value of the set
- Counts by touching and partitioning
- Counts by pointing
- Subitises for small quantities

Children respond well to questions such as:

- Have we enough?
- Who has more/fewer?

especially where they have been encouraged to respond using the mathematical vocabulary that they hear the adults using. Gradually they begin to respond in sentences and this should be encouraged.

What three and four year olds find more difficult are questions which ask 'How do you know?' such as:

- How can you be sure that you have counted them all?

Here the children tend not to respond. PGCE students trialled some of the key questions in 2001 and discovered that young children did not cope well with this sort of question. However, with practice, and with examples of how they might answer given by adults, they do begin to answer the 'How do you know?' type of question in a satisfactory way.

Errors in counting

There are documented (Baroody, 1987; Gelman and Gallistel, 1986), common misconceptions and difficulties which children encounter with counting. These can be summarised as:

- counting one, two, three, then any number or name to represent 'many';
- number names not remembered in rote order;
- counting pattern not stable, that is, when counting children produce counting names out of sequence;
- counting not sequenced with the partition;
- count does not stop when the partition is completed;
- counts one item more than once, or not at all.

For all these errors, children will benefit from more experience of counting, using a range of different contexts. All adults in the nursery should be aware of which children are experiencing difficulties with counting and what types of errors they make and which experiences will be needed to help the child to increase their counting fluency when counting opportunities arise in the child's play. Similarly, where there is clear evidence of the errors that individual children make when counting, focused activities can be planned to give further, specific experience of counting.

It should be remembered that in English children need to learn ten discrete number names, then order them, in order to be able to count from one to ten. Once children begin to count beyond ten, our English number names are confusing. We say eleven, twelve, thirteen . . . There is no discernable pattern of naming the numbers here, nor of helping the children to understand what these numbers mean. However, other languages, including Asian languages, utilise a system which refers to numbers after ten as *ten-one, ten-two* . . .; then *two-ten, two-ten-one* . . . and so on. Children will benefit from having many opportunities to say number names in order, and, as they mature, to count beyond ten, so that those patterns become secure.

Joseph was six years old and had just learnt to count beyond twenty. He was in a class of children who were a year younger than him, in order to provide him with further early literacy and mathematical experiences. He announced one morning, 'I can do it!' and was asked to count for all of the children to hear. All went well at first: *eighteen, nineteen, twenty, twenty-one, twenty-two,* . . . And then *twenty-eight, twenty-nine, twenty-ten, twenty-eleven* . . . Joseph had learned that the number patterns repeat. What he still had not figured out was how the number names changed with the new decade.

1.7 Working in partnership with parents and carers

Parents often give invaluable help in the nursery on a regular basis. In Section 1.5 above, the importance of involving all adults in the planning was stressed. For partnership between home and nursery to develop effectively, many parents will welcome opportunities to work with their children at home, reinforcing and extending the experiences which their children have had during the day. To support the partnership, some nurseries have set up lending libraries of books, toys and games which parents organise for themselves.

Activities for counting at home

These activities do not require any special equipment, as they make use of everyday items in the home.

Counting everyday things at home:

- the cans of baked beans to go into the cupboard; the carrots into the rack; the apples into the fruit dish.
- all the red cars; all the play people; the bricks as they go away; the stairs on the way to bed.
- enough plates for everyone for dinner; biscuits for each child; fish fingers onto the plates; enough for everyone to have a sweet.

Counting on the way to nursery:

- the houses along the street; the cars that go past; the trees in the garden; the windows in that house; the chimneys on the roof.

Counting when out shopping:

- coins for paying for goods; all the pennies; the postage stamps for the letters; how many cakes for tea; enough oranges for everyone to have one.

Counting games which can be played at home

These can be game packs for lending to parents, or homes may already have these. Again, they do not require sophisticated equipment, relying upon playing cards, boards, dice and dominoes.

- *Snap:* matching for sameness. This can be limited by using playing cards 1 to 5 from each set and counting the pips. Special snap picture cards can be purchased from toy shops, or ordinary playing cards can be used.
- *Pelmanism:* snap cards or ordinary playing cards can be used. The cards can be placed face down either in rows or in a random arrangement, and two are turned over each time. When matching quantities are found, the player keeps that pair. The winner has the most pairs of matching cards.
- *Lotto:* picture lotto, where the items in the pictures can be counted, gives good experience of pointing and counting pictures. Children can be encouraged to count the pictures again, starting with a different item as 'one'.
- *Dominoes:* children match the ends of dominoes for 'sameness' (Figure 1.4).

Figure 1.4 Domino match

- *Board games with a dice:* children match the number on the dice with physically counting along the board's track. Ludo and other simple track games can be played.

CHAPTER 2

Number

The *Curriculum Guidance for the Foundation Stage* (DfEE, 2000) identifies the following key objectives for children to reach by the end of the reception stage:

- Recognise numerals 1 to 9.
- In practical activities and discussion begin to use the vocabulary involved in adding and subtracting.
- Use language such as 'more' and 'less' to compare two numbers.
- Find one more than or one less than a number from one to ten.
- Begin to relate addition to combining two groups of objects and subtraction to 'taking away'.
- Use developing mathematical ideas and methods to solve practical problems.

The Early Learning Goals' Stepping Stones in the *Curriculum Guidance for the Foundation Stage* (DfEE, 2000) show the developmental stages which children need in order to be able to meet the key objectives. The activity ideas within this chapter will help practitioners to develop children's understanding in the above aspects of number.

Counting has been considered in depth in the previous chapter, and is an essential component of developing the concepts and skills as outlined above. The concepts and skills associated with counting develop alongside understanding about number.

2.1 The mathematics

Ordering

Through their counting experiences and from their growing understanding of equivalence (Chapter 1), young children begin to understand that where there is inequivalence, that is, where two sets do not have the same cardinal value, there is an order relationship between the two sets. Gelman and Gallistel (1986) found that most young children did not use the mathematical language of more and fewer, but they still demonstrated that they understood the concept through making sets to fit the ordering pattern.

Through using language such as 'more', 'the same', and 'fewer', children make comparisons between the cardinal aspect of number and the ordinal aspect. This is number used in a different sense from the cardinal, and the same number names are used for both concepts. As children count, they use ordinal number (one, two, three . . .) using the names in a pre-determined order, and the last number in the count defines the cardinal aspect of their count. Ordinal number is used frequently in everyday life. Children use ordinal number in their play:

- Running toy cars down a slope, the red car wins (first) and the blue car is last (third).
- Counting the sheep (one), then the cow (two), then the pig (three) gives an order to their counting to arrive at the cardinal value of 'three'.
- Dressing teddy: first the vest, then his pants and last is his jumper.

Baroody (1987) suggested that finger counting may play an important role in the development of understanding ordinal and cardinal number. Children count one, two, three . . . using their fingers and see that, with the increasing order of the numbers, the cardinal value increases, and that two is one more than one, three is one more than two, and so on. Ordinal number also has its own set of words to be learnt, first, second . . . last. Making sense of ordinal, as well as cardinal number, is essential to developing understanding of how numbers work, especially in beginning to develop understanding of the number operations of addition and subtraction.

Kate, aged four years six months, counted the fingers of her left hand, pointing with her right. She started with her thumb. 'One, two, three, four, five. It always comes to five. This one (index finger) is two.' Her mother suggested that she start with her little finger and count again. 'One, two, three, four, five. It's still five. And now this one (index finger) is four.' Kate could not consistently count all ten fingers. She was unable to switch from pointing with one hand to pointing with the other.

The use of a number line in the setting helps children to see the order of the numerals. By counting along the number line, they begin to relate the reading of the number with its spoken word. They also begin to make mental images of the numbers, of their place within the order of numbers, and also of how to read, and then to begin to write them. Children benefit from having access to a number line during play (Carruthers, 1997; Pound, 1999). Number lines can include clothes pegs with numbers hanging from the clothes line or magnetic numbers. Children should be encouraged to place numerals onto the number line, in order. Similarly they can play games with numeral cards, taking turns to place a card on the table until all of the cards have been ordered.

Early concepts of addition and subtraction

The status quo

It has long been held in Britain, that young children are not 'ready' to begin number operations until they can conserve number, and that, following Piaget's stages of development, this understanding does not develop until the child reaches the concrete operational stage at about seven years of age. This has had a major influence upon the nursery number curriculum, in that it has been considered quite inappropriate for young children to engage with addition and subtraction, as they are not, in Piaget's view, able to conserve a quantity, and thus cannot break down two quantities, combine them and identify how many in total (Hughes, 1986).

This view has been challenged by research from Hughes (1986) where he showed that by the time children start school, many of them can add and subtract, in context, with small numbers. These research findings are in direct conflict with the advice of Geoffrey and Julia Matthews (1978; third edition, 1990): 'There is so much to learn, before the simplest calculations can have any meaning, that the idea of "sums for the very young child" is ludicrous.' This advice is given together with their suggestions that a nursery curriculum for mathematics should emphasise matching, sorting, comparing and ordering and that invariance (conservation) of number can be introduced but that children will be too young (the Piagetian view) to understand this concept fully. The Matthews view was reinforced through the publication of the Nuffield Mathematics Project (1970), which influenced reception and Key Stage 1 teaching, emphasising the importance of sorting, matching and comparing, rather than using these as contexts for counting.

Through the Foundation Curriculum, the DfEE (2000) has taken the view that early operations such as addition and subtraction, which young children are already developing, should be encouraged through the nursery mathematics curriculum, and this implies that there will need to be reconsideration of the way in which such concepts and skills are taught through mainstream schools' planning and use of published mathematics schemes, as the implication is that children will enter mainstream education at five years of age with some ability to add and subtract with small numbers in meaningful contexts.

Research findings

Through their developing counting skills, young children begin to see how number quantities can be changed (Baroody, 1987). Experiences such as: 'count out two biscuits . . . and one more . . . and now there are three' and, 'count out three biscuits . . . and eat one . . . and there are two' allow children to explore increasing and decreasing by one and to begin to understand how numbers can be changed by counting one more or one fewer. Children, through their experience, begin to answer with accuracy what 'one more' will be, and similarly 'one fewer'. This can be summarised as being able to respond to $N+1$ and $N-1$ situations, or number after N and number before N.

What nursery-aged children found much more difficult was to respond to $1+N$. This is more difficult because children may see, for example $1+2$ as 1 and 2 more, and not realise that $N+1=1+N$ (the commutativity law). However, with experience, and by the time they enter mainstream school, many children have realised that $1+N$ can be solved by using the one more than N rule.

Through the $N-1$ experiences children will meet the concept of zero, of nothing left. Gelman and Gallistel (1986) suggest that when counting sets there is no need for a zero as there is nothing to count in the empty set. Zero arises either as a consequence of subtraction, when, for example, there are two marbles in the pot, and both are taken out, and nothing remains; or of finding nothing, such as opening a box and finding that it is empty. Zero has cardinal and ordinal value. It is (cardinal) the empty set. Its ordinal value is special; it comes before one on the number line, is often the starting point for counting on a number line and is used to represent midnight on a digital watch, freezing point on a Celsius thermometer, and ground floor on some lifts (Haylock and Cockburn, 1989). Zero is not just the concept of nothing, but also represents a place in the number line before negative numbers. Children will meet negative numbers as soon as they explore arithmetic using a calculator, such as $3-4=-1$. Perhaps difficulty with the concept of zero is compounded by the range of vocabulary used to express the concept: 'zero', 'nothing', 'nought', 'empty set'; other numbers have just one name. These words will be used in their own context, that is, for a number line children will say zero, for the empty box they will say empty or nothing, for the written 0 they will say zero or perhaps nought. The concept of zero can be introduced through both its aspects: as the empty set, its cardinal value; and as the number before one in the counting sequence, for example in a count-down from ten: ten, nine, eight . . . two, one, zero.

Hughes' (1986) experiments with nursery-age children and their fluency with addition and subtraction revealed some new findings. He placed some small bricks into a box, with the child watching and counting, but without the child being able to see the bricks inside the box. He asked how many were in the box, then let the child count to check; he added one or two bricks, or removed one or two, and asked again how many there were and the child responded without being able to see the bricks.

Hughes found that in solving these problems the children used two different strategies, depending upon whether small numbers up to four or five were used, or larger quantities. For smaller numbers he found that children either just named the amount or counted out aloud from one until they arrived at their result. He believed that they formed an image or representation of the bricks in the box. Some children counted on their fingers. Others seemed to form a visual image of the bricks inside the box, tapping their finger at different places along the box as if 'seeing' the bricks and counting them. For larger quantities and addition they counted on, from the initial quantity, so that for five and two more, they counted 'five, six, seven'; and for subtraction they counted back from the initial quantity, 'eight, seven, six'. As Hughes pointed out this is quite a complex procedure, as children need to keep a mental tally of the counting on or back steps that they take. Counting on and counting back had not been taught as a strategy and was one which children seemed to develop for themselves.

Hughes also asked hypothetical questions about the bricks, such as 'If there was one brick in the box and I added two more, how many would there be?' and found that for small numbers, they found this a harder problem than for larger numbers. He hypothesised that this could be to do with the different strategies which children adopted to solve the problems when there were bricks in the box, and that if they construct a mental image of the bricks in the box, then having the box in front of them might help, whereas with counting on and back, the sight of the box does not help. He asked the questions without the imagery of the bricks, for example, 'What does one and two make?' or What does two take away one make?' and found that most of the children were unable to respond correctly. He suggested that this was not a lack of understanding of arithmetic, but a difficulty in translating between their concrete experiences and the formal language of addition and subtraction. He suggested that children could be helped to form the bridge between the concrete and the formal, abstract language by using their fingers to represent the numerical quantities.

Groen and Resnick (1977) found that children aged about five could be taught counting on strategies to solve simple addition problems and that more than half the study group switched from mentally counting all the objects to counting on from the larger number. Hughes' (1986) later research suggests that this is a strategy which can be encouraged in much younger children so that by the time they enter mainstream school they will have begun to develop effective counting on and back strategies for solving simple, contextualised addition and subtraction problems. This suggests that the traditional methods for teaching addition and subtraction in the early years in school will need to be reviewed, as so many children are taught to count out, say, three cubes, then two, then put them together and count all.

The overall message from these research findings is that young children can and do use and understand addition and subtraction, as long as the numbers are kept small and are used in contexts which have meaning to them and that they find interesting. Nursery-age children have the ability to use and understand addition and subtraction, in context, but teaching how to do formal, written, pages of sums is unlikely to be successful, as these would be abstract and without meaning.

Sara, two years six months, and Jake, three years two months (see Section 1.4), had discussed how many buttons they had:

Jake: You've got more than me.
Sara: More.
Jake: Yes. I've got three and you've got two. I've got one more.

Following their discussion an adult asked Jake and Sara to open their hands. This confirmed that they had three and two buttons respectively. She asked Jake to explain how he knew that he had one more button than Sara:

Jake: Well, you see, Sara had one and I had four and that's five altogether and I gave Sara one of mine 'cos she wanted more and now she's got two and I've got three.

This was quite a complex piece of mental arithmetic. Jake was able to add and subtract, in context, for small amounts up to five.

Children's understanding of subtraction is usually 'take away' at this stage. There are two other forms which children will meet during Key Stage 1, of difference and complementary addition. It is possible, from the findings of Hughes (1986), and Gelman and Gallistel (1986), which show that children do use counting on and back strategies as well as taking away, that difference is beginning to be understood. Jake, in the above example, demonstrated that he understood one more, that is, a difference of one, rather than 'take away'. More recent research (cited in Baroody, 2000) shows that at some point children abandon using objects and rely instead on verbal counting procedures. So, for example, for the problem *Said helped to decorate five cakes before lunch. After lunch he decorated three more cakes. How many cakes did he help to decorate altogether?* the child may count up to five, *one, two, three, four, five,* and then count three more *six, seven, eight.* The child may use their fingers to help to make the total. If the language of difference (counting on and back, making comparisons, using more, fewer) and of complementary addition (counting on to the larger number from the smaller) is encouraged where it occurs in children's thinking, then these concepts will be more readily understood during Key Stage 1. However, for many children it is the symbolic recording of both take away and difference as a subtraction statement, and the same formal recording being used for both concepts, which causes confusion.

Early concepts of division, fractions and multiplication

Division, multiplication and fractions are not mentioned specifically in the Foundation Curriculum. However, everyday activities involve the use of fractions, and division; for example, sharing out pieces of fruit at snack time and making sure everyone has a fair share; and cutting up the birthday cake so that everyone has a similar sized piece. In this section, children's ability to use simple sharing and fraction experiences will be considered, as will the place of multiplication in the nursery curriculum. Parents may teach their children to count; there is no evidence to suggest that they teach their children how to divide, multiply or make equal parts of numbers (fractions). In some cultures fraction language, with its precise mathematical meaning, has not developed in the way that it has in western societies; in some societies, fraction words exist, but they have less precise meaning, so that societies such as Papua New Guinea have a word for 'half' which in fact means 'a piece' or 'a part' (Lean, 1988). In reviewing the literature of children's number acquisition, there is nothing to suggest that children gain explicit understanding of these operations prior to starting mainstream school. However, the following observations would challenge that view.

Sharing

Sharing is one form of division. It is defined in Haylock and Cockburn (1989) as putting objects into groups, so for example, 6÷3 is three groups of two. Children in the nursery sharing items between bowls in the home area will compare whether the bowls have fair shares, whether one has more than the others (particularly if they are sharing out things to eat!) and they will find that sometimes quantities cannot be shared fairly, because there is a remainder. Three year olds share using the dealing method of one for you and one for me. They do not usually then count to check that they have each received a fair share. Other children may just move their hands through some items, and give one part to a friend and keep one part for themselves, without any consideration of whether they each have the same quantity (Geist, 2001; Pepper and Hunting, 1998). Pepper and Hunting's research showed that, even when children cannot yet count systematically, they can still engage in sharing activities where they use the dealing system, or a variation of that. Through sharing activities the language of fractions may be used; for example, in sharing out playing cards or dominoes, so that each player has 'half'.

Fractions

In an Australian research project Hunting and Sharpley (1988) compared three to five year old children's use of fraction language. They found that, through the use of practical sharing tasks, most of those studied could share equally between two dolls, and many of them between three and four dolls. When fraction language such as 'half', 'quarter', 'third', was used, hardly any of the children responded correctly. Similarly, Clements and Del Campo (1990) showed that children aged six to ten who could share equally did not necessarily understand and respond correctly to the fraction terms 'one half', 'one quarter', 'one third'. They suggest that the study of fractions 'is not natural, and is needed only for the purpose of studying more mathematics'. However, in western culture and languages, fraction language is used in a social sense as well as having mathematical meaning and this is a use of fractions which nursery-age children develop, given appropriate experiences. The following conversation took place in a 45-place nursery school, between four children aged about four and a visitor.

Jane: Will you come on a picnic with us?
Visitor: Yes, please.
Jane: Here we are.

Jane points to a carpeted area, with two other children, a table-top made by using the base of an upturned garage, some school dinner knives and forks, a saucepan which contains raw, peeled carrots and potatoes.

Kim: We're cutting up the vegetables to have for our picnic. Do you like it here in our wood?
Jane: Yes, we've been to the circus and now we're going to have our picnic dinner. Now let me see. You have half of this carrot and I'll have half.

Visitor: What are Kim and Peter going to eat?

Jane: Oh, they have half of this carrot (proceeds to cut it into two unidentical pieces).

Visitor: Can everyone have a piece of this carrot?

Jane: Quarters. Yes, I'll cut it up.

Discussions with the staff in the nursery revealed that raw vegetables had been placed in the kitchen area on three successive days so that they could observe what the children would do with them. The staff had observed the children, responded to their play by helping them to extend their language, and the language of fractions had arisen because the children wanted to share out cut-up pieces of vegetables.

Whilst the formal, mathematical concept of fractions would be quite inappropriate at this stage, the social sense in which fractions can be used can form part of the nursery curriculum. The language of fractions may occur naturally, in a measuring context, such as pouring out half a cup of water, cutting a piece of string in half, or folding a cloth in half and then into quarters (and see Chapter 5, Measuring). It must be remembered that children will probably not understand that two halves must be the same size and that they will probably want the 'biggest half'! (Althouse, 1994).

Repeated subtraction

Imagine that there is a plate of eight biscuits. Four children are told that they may take two biscuits each. The plate can be passed around the group until everyone has received their biscuits and there are none left. This is an experience of division by repeated subtraction. If there had been nine biscuits then there would have been a remainder and children would begin to realise that there are occasions when everyone has fair shares and other occasions when there are either not enough or some left after everyone has had their fair share. Similarly, in singing number rhymes which count back in twos, e.g. 'Ten fat sausages sizzling in a pan', 'There were ten in the bed', children experience repeated subtraction, observing two fewer fingers held up for each verse.

The link between division and fractions at this stage is one of using the mathematical language of sharing, repeated subtraction, and fractions in a social setting. This stems from common experiences in a nursery setting, where children can be encouraged to put items in groups, to consider what is fair when sharing out items, use language of 'half' and possibly 'quarter' and to count backwards in twos. This gives children the beginnings of ideas of division, which they will meet more formally in their early years in mainstream school.

Multiplication

Multiplication is a more difficult concept to introduce as there are no natural occurrences where it is used in the nursery, nor commonly known rhymes where the counting is in repeated additions of, for example, twos, fives or tens. Multiplication is not useful to children of this age, and through multiplication the quantity soon increases to an amount which is outside their counting skills, and would have little meaning other than 'lots'. Gelman and Gallistel (1986) saw multiplication as a development from counting, when repeatedly counting large numbers of objects becomes difficult to control. This is not a situation which arises naturally for a three or four year old, who will be unlikely to need to count such large amounts.

It would be possible to teach children to count in twos, fives and tens as a rote exercise at this stage. However, there is no value in such rote learning at this stage, especially when there is so much in mathematics which is exciting and of immediate use to three and four year olds, and as the nursery curriculum already makes such demands upon the available time this cannot be justified.

Larger numbers

Introduction to numbers in the nursery curriculum has, usually, until quite recently, been limited to counting numbers to ten. In commercial mathematics schemes, the size of number which four and five year olds meet once they have started mainstream education is often limited to numbers to ten, such as in *Nelson Mathematics* (Domoney *et al.*, 1991). The High Scope number curriculum (Hohmann *et al.*, 1978) takes a traditional Piagetian view, the introduction of small counting numbers and no mention of larger numbers or environmental numbers. In *Early Mathematical Experiences* (Matthews and Matthews, 1990), again the Piagetian view of how children learn about number is espoused, and although there is a chapter called The Environment larger numbers are not mentioned through the topics developed such as Shopping and Houses.

When larger numbers are introduced in mainstream school, often this can be in isolation from their meanings. Children will learn about place value, perhaps by bundling straws or using base ten apparatus. Numbers have meaning through their context; for example, an average serving of rice (50 g before cooking) would contain about 2000 grains; a million grains of rice is not such a large mound of rice, about 25 kg, or 25 packs of rice stacked on the supermarket shelf; a large (750 g) packet of cornflakes would contain about 7500 flakes of corn and a million flakes of corn would weigh approximately 100 kg. Where numbers have no context, they have no meaning other than just as a number. Children enjoy large numbers; they enjoy speculating on thousands, millions, and what these mean in particular contexts.

All around them, nursery-age children will see larger numbers used as part of everyday life, such as car number plates, house numbers, bus numbers, telephone numbers, video displays, clocks, prices in shop windows, lottery numbers on television on Saturday evenings, and so on. They may play board and card games at home with older brothers and sisters (Bergeron and Herscovics, 1990). They may handle money and name the coins using numbers: 20p, 50p. Numbers in everyday use are used in three different ways and are not limited to 10: cardinal (how many); ordinal (position) and nominal (as a name, such as the 137 bus). Van Oers (1997) noted how children use nominal number to name things, for example, using the number 43 as a label for a boat in a drawing. Through their everyday experiences children have rich opportunities to observe and discuss numbers which are much larger than traditionally would have been used in nursery education.

Within the nursery environment, numbers should be on display in different contexts, such as a simple telephone directory for children to use (Figure 2.1). The role play situations of the shop, café, hairdressers . . . all give opportunities for children to use money, mirroring situations in everyday life, and thus the opportunity to become familiar with and use larger numbers than ten.

Telephone Numbers

Nursery   123

Shop   456

Doctor   789

Police   999

Figure 2.1 A telephone directory display

Recording

In the UK, children are not traditionally introduced to the written symbols for numbers until they begin to learn formal arithmetic, which is usually expressed in the abstract form of numbers and signs and out of any context, such as $3+5=8$. Traditionally, the nursery curriculum did not include the recording of numbers. However, with the growth of understanding of the principles of emergent writing (Clipson-Boyles, 1996), and with the evidence from the work of Hughes (1986) on children's own inventions of recording numbers, there is now firm evidence that nursery-age children can record their mathematics and 'read' what they have written in a systematic way.

In his research Hughes (1986) asked children aged three to seven years to 'put something on paper' to show how many bricks there were. Children responded in one of four ways:

- *Idiosyncratic response* (Figure 2.2). Here children made marks on the paper that had no meaningful pattern to the adult observer. Hughes noted that these marks may have had meaning to the child. Amanda, two years five months, wrote a shopping list for her mother. She discussed what was to be bought and made marks on the paper. However, she could not 'read' her writing nor explain how many each mark represented.
- *Pictographic response* (Figure 2.3). Here a picture symbol was used to represent each item, such as square shapes for bricks. These pictures are in one-to-one correspondence with the items being counted.

- *Iconic response*. This is also one-to-one correspondence, usually using tally marks, though Hughes found that some children drew a picture such as a circle or house to represent each brick. The number of tallies usually matched the number of objects.
- *Symbolic response*. In this case the children wrote numerals or, in a few cases, number words, to represent the quantity of bricks. The numeral or number word did not always match the count.

Figure 2.2 Idiosyncratic recording of a shopping list by Amanda, aged two years two months

Hughes noted that many of the pre-school children used iconic responses to the task, rather than idiosyncratic responses. He noted that the tally marks could be regarded as similar to finger counting, which many young children in his experience could already use. When Hughes asked children to represent zero, or nothing, those who used symbolic recording usually responded with 0. Those who had used iconic or pictographic responses in representing bricks, had a range of responses to this. Some used 0, others a dash or a dot; some drew an empty box, some a single brick or tally mark. Many children found the representation of nothing puzzling.

Hughes invented the 'tin game' where he asked children aged between three years one month and five years ten months to make marks on tins to show how many bricks were inside. The tins held one, two or three bricks or were empty. He

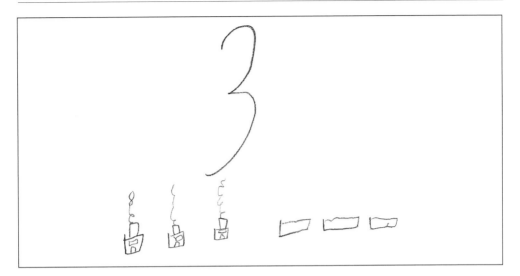

Figure 2.3 Nathaniel (four years eight months), showed three ways of recording '3': pictographic, iconic and symbolic

found that the children could mark the tins in such a way that they could 'read' their marks, stating how many were in each tin, including the empty one, on a follow-up session a week later. He followed this experiment with one where children aged five to nine were asked to record addition and subtraction of bricks and discovered that none of those in the study chose to use the conventional signs of +, −, and =. He concluded that their use of the symbols in the classroom seemed to apply just to the classroom context and did not transfer to other situations.

Hughes' research shows that nursery-age children can record quantities in a meaningful way. Where children see adults writing numbers which have meaning, or making other marks such as tallies, or using pictograms to represent quantities, they will come to understand that these have meaning and begin to make their own marks, whether pictographic, iconic, or symbolic. Numerals need to be used in contexts in the nursery, such as number friezes, number lines, displays which include numbers, counting books with numbers and pictures, and the shop with prices displayed, so that numerals are seen as a method of recording. Making writing materials available, and asking adults working in the setting to record numbers, will encourage children to try this for themselves.

As children's experience of numerical concepts grows, so significant connections are made in understanding (Haylock and Cockburn, 1989) (Figure 2.4):

- using materials and equipment in practical situations;
- listening to and using appropriately new mathematical vocabulary;
- recording the mathematical situation pictorially;
- using symbolic recording to express the mathematics.

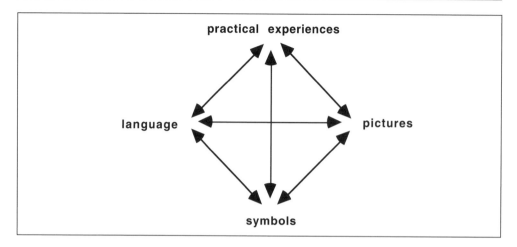

Figure 2.4 Inter-relationships in understanding mathematics, with acknowledgement to Haylock and Cockburn (1989)

Problem-solving

Problem-solving skills develop through experience of working on practical problems. These are problems which show a real need, and require real solutions, and not the traditional word or symbolic problems of 'How much is five sweets and two more sweets?' or '5+2'.

For three and four year old children, much of their work during nursery is about solving problems. They might plan to make a robot from junk materials, deciding how many pieces of junk they will need; they might decide to share out some pretend food in the home area and wonder how many pieces they can give to each child; they might be asked to find three large paintbrushes and two small and count how many they have altogether. All of these experiences are problems to be solved by the nursery child. Many of the problems which the children attempt to solve are self-set. Adults will be involved in discussion, questioning and perhaps asking 'what if?' questions to help the child to seek an improved solution. Problems may be short tasks, ones that can be resolved in moments. Others may be extended tasks which will take a morning to solve and perhaps be returned to over the next few days, while the children look for alternative solutions. Some problems may involve just one child; others may involve a group working together to find a solution.

Studies have shown that children aged four to five years tend to tackle a problem without having considered the strategies required which will lead to success (Askew and Williams, 1995). In High Scope nurseries, where children are encouraged to plan what they want to do and how they might go about it (Hohmann *et al.*, 1978), adults encourage the children to review these plans on a regular basis so that the children evaluate the quality of their work and its success and, as they come to understand the process, to refine their plans. This leads to improved problem-solving strategies being used. High Scope nurseries refer to the Plan–Do–Review cycle, and this fits well with the Problem Solving and Enquiry strand of the Scottish mathematics curriculum (SOED, 1991) which has three stages:

- *Starting a task:* this involves understanding the problem and deciding how to proceed.
- *Doing a task:* using appropriate approaches and materials, drawing a picture, trying out different possible strategies to find one that works.
- *Reporting on a task:* reviewing what has been done; deciding if there might be a better way of solving the problem; identifying extensions to the problem.

These three stages match closely the strands in Key Stage 1, Using and Applying Mathematics, of the English Mathematics National Curriculum for Key Stage 1 (DfE, 1995):

- making and monitoring decisions to solve problems;
- developing mathematical language and communication;
- developing mathematical reasoning.

It therefore seems reasonable to look at the skills associated with problem-solving for the National Curriculum and to identify those which would be appropriate for nursery-age children to begin to develop, through solving real, practical problems. The following are suggested, and have been developed from SOED (1991), DfE (1995) and from the *Non-Statutory Guidance for Mathematics* (National Curriculum Council 1989).

- *Making a plan.* This will be a verbal plan, describing what they plan to do. Children can be encouraged to draw a picture or record numbers using pictographic, iconic or symbolic notation.
- *Selecting materials* to use for solving the problem. In many cases, the problem will be concerned with particular materials, and thus the materials are already selected. In other cases, the children may decide upon the materials to use, such as using pennies in the shop, or choosing paper and pencil to write a shopping list.
- *Estimating.* Developing skills of estimation can be encouraged through children making a 'guess' and checking by counting, by responding to questions such as 'Do you think that there will be enough for everyone to have one?' or 'How many bricks do you think there are in that tower? Shall we check by counting them?'
- *Using their growing knowledge of number* to help them to solve the problem, such as knowing that there are three bears and only two chairs so that there are insufficient chairs for the bears; or putting two play people in the car, and asking for two more to fill the spaces because it holds four play people.
- *Discussing the progress of the task.* Adult intervention in children's problem-solving should encourage the children to discuss what they are doing, to review how well it is going and whether there might be alternative strategies to try; for example, when sharing out biscuits, questions such as 'Are there enough for everyone? How can you tell?' or when making a truck from a construction kit, 'How many wheels will you need? Are there enough in the box?'

- *Evaluating the effectiveness of the outcome.* Discussion with adults will encourage children to compare their original planning with the finished outcome. Similarly discussion between children should be encouraged. They can review what worked well and consider other options which they might follow. The more confident child can be encouraged to continue with the task, trying out other strategies, such as sharing out a different quantity of biscuits to see if everyone can still have one; or making another, different structure using the same number of bricks; or making a different threaded bead pattern, using three red beads and two blue beads, then four red beads and three blue beads. Adults and children can ask 'What if . . .?' questions to explore other possibilities.

Throughout their mathematical work, children will need to be encouraged to develop positive attitudes towards their learning and enjoyment from the mathematics. These attitudes can be summarised as (NCC, 1989):

- being willing to tackle the problem, to 'have a go';
- trying out alternative strategies;
- persevering, even when it is difficult to resolve a problem;
- working with others, in collaboration;
- being willing to put forward a different viewpoint or possible solution.

2.2 Key concepts

The number concepts considered in this chapter should be considered as building upon the counting experiences detailed in Chapter 1, and integral to the counting experiences. Experiences which encourage the development of addition and subtraction skills will also involve counting and possibly children's own recording. Those which consider larger numbers will probably include written numerals and children's own recording. The key concepts can be summarised as follows.

Ordering

- Begin to use the language of ordering, such as one more than, first, second . . . last.

When counting out items, children can be encouraged to explore ordinal number, by counting out three, then four, and comparing to see that four is one more than three. During circle time, when counting songs and rhymes are sung, children will experience counting both forwards and backwards, which will reinforce the order of the counting numbers. If counting rhymes which involve finger actions are used, then children can compare how many fingers are held up for 'two' and that one more is needed for 'three'. For birthdays, the concept of 'one more than' is appropriate, one year older, one more candle on the cake. If children are learning to recognise numerals, then a washing line with numerals pegged to it in order can be used as a focused activity with a small group (Figure 2.5). (See Focused

Activities, p. 50.) Similarly the washing line and numerals can be used to play games where numerals are pegged, in numerical order.

Figure 2.5 Number lines help children to recognise numerals

Addition and subtraction

- Know that N+1 is one more than N and N−1 is one fewer than N.
- Develop strategies such as finger counting and mental imagery, for addition and subtraction of small quantities.
- Begin to relate addition to combining two groups of objects, and subtraction to 'taking away'.
- Begin to make reasonable estimates of small quantities.
- Recognise and use appropriate language to describe zero, both cardinal and ordinal aspects.

Children will begin to use addition and subtraction to describe number situations, particularly in response to sensitive adult intervention.

Tara says: There are two dolls in the bed and two in the cot. They can sit on the chairs. (Child points to four chairs at the table.)

Sam makes patterns on a pegboard, using four pegs.
'What if each pattern had two colours?' Sam changes one of them, using one red and three blue. He explains 'Three and one is four. I can do this one too. Look.' He changes it to two green and two red.

In the shop, Gavin says 'That is 2p and 1p. That's 3p please' and Hannah counts out three pennies.

As children begin to explore addition and subtraction so they can be encouraged to use mental imagery. For example, they may count, pointing and touching with their finger, then move to just pointing. With more abstract problems, such as Gavin in the shop example above, children may begin to use a mental image of a number line to solve such problems. A floor number track is useful to encourage this, as children can jump or step along the track, and look at how far they have moved. 'Let's start on three. Now jump along to five. How many jumps did you make?'

Ideas about addition and subtraction will also be developed through the use of materials. For example, counting all the red bricks, then the blue bricks, then counting all of them leads to an understanding of 'There are three blue bricks and two red ones. There are five bricks altogether.' Similarly, with subtraction as 'taking away' children can use materials to model this. 'I have five sheep. I'll give you two. Now I have three left.'

Estimation can be encouraged, during a focused activity, by covering a few items on a tray with a cloth so that their outline shows clearly. Children make a 'guess' and then the cloth is removed for them to count to check. Similarly, asking children to take a handful of items such as buttons or large counters and to guess how many they have, then to count will help them to improve the accuracy of their estimation. Zero, nothing, nought, empty, can be introduced during adult intervention, particularly if all the items from a box, for example, have been removed. The ordinal aspects could be used as a count-down for an event:

> The children hold their buggies, ready to let them run down the slope all at the same time to see which one goes the furthest. 'Five, four, three, two, one, zero!' and the buggies run away.

Division, fractions and multiplication

- Make fair shares of a quantity.
- Use language of division, such as share, fair, same, and fractions such as half.

Sharing activities will normally occur as part of a social event, such as sharing out food and drinks at snack time. The sharing at this stage will probably be one item at a time around the group, repeated until all the items have been given out. Where children have their snack in a small group, the adult can discuss the sharing out with them, using language such as fair, enough, the same, one left over. Fraction language can be introduced whilst children are, for example, cutting up dough, sharing out dominoes to play a game, or folding a cloth:

> That's a long clay sausage! Will you give me half?
> How many pieces are there now?

How many bricks are there?
Tom would like half of them.
How many have you? How many has Tom?
You have half each.

Larger numbers

- Name some larger numbers such as telephone number, house number (Figure 2.6).
- Recognise contexts where larger numbers are used, such as in shopping and on car number plates.

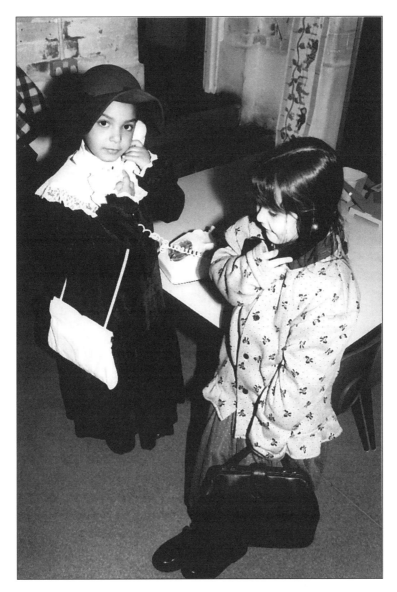

Figure 2.6 Neila and Lisa dialled each other's home telephone numbers prior to their telephone conversation

On their way to nursery, children will encounter numbers in the environment, such as on road signs, petrol pumps, shop windows and doors. Those who are beginning to recognise numerals can make a scrap book of numbers from magazine photographs and packaging. Within the nursery, there are many opportunities to display numbers, both small and larger ones. In the doctor's surgery, there could be a clock, an appointments book, posters with prices for baby foods, a height chart, thermometer and dial weighing scales. A collection of photographs of front doors or car number plates could show larger numbers.

If small groups of children are taken out of the nursery, perhaps to go to the local shop, they can be encouraged on their walk to look for numbers. When they return, with the help of an adult, they can make a list of all the places where they saw numbers, and of any numbers that they remember.

Recording

- Make a record of numbers, using a pictographic, iconic or symbolic response.
- Name some numerals.

As children become aware that print has meaning, there will be opportunities to encourage them to recognise and name numerals. A number frieze, clearly displayed, will give children a point of reference for identifying numerals. Number friezes do not have to be displayed on a wall. Instead, jars with one, two, three . . . items in and the appropriate numeral on the outside can be put on a table, for children to order and to use as a reference. Children can cut out numerals to make sets of 'the same', such as a set of 'fours'. They can draw numerals in the sand; paint numerals; and decorate large numerals with collage.

When role playing children should be encouraged to make a written record, such as a shopping list which shows how many tins of baked beans to buy, or a list which shows how many doughnuts have been ordered in the café. At first, the recording may be idiosyncratic, but with encouragement, they will use pictographic, iconic or symbolic recording. Children will benefit from seeing examples of recording around the nursery which use tallies or pictures, such as a record of how many lettuce leaves or carrots the rabbits were fed each day, or a tally showing how many children had birthdays that week.

Problem-solving

- Plan, carry out and review problem-solving tasks.
- Choose suitable materials for the task.
- Respond to 'what if . . .?' questions through further problem-solving activity.
- Use mathematical language when discussing the work.

Problem-solving will be part of everyday nursery life. Children should be encouraged to use their growing understanding of number in order to help them to solve problems. The review of the task, whether undertaken between the child and adult, or in a small group with other children offering comments and advice, is important as it encourages reflection on the plan and its effectiveness as well as encouraging children to consider whether what they planned to do was what they actually did. The discussion before they begin a larger task, where children consider possible strategies, will help them to begin to realise that there may be more than one way of approaching the task. These are sophisticated skills and concepts. What is intended is that through this approach children will become more confident in their ability to use their growing knowledge about number to solve problems.

These number concepts are interdependent, and all rely upon the children's growing skill with counting. During their work, children may be exploring more than one of these concepts at any time.

Concept map (Table 2.1)

This shows the concepts outlined above in matrix form, together with examples of vocabulary which can be developed. Some example activities are shown in order to demonstrate how these concepts might be explored in a nursery setting. The map can be used as a basis for planning. Some assessment checkpoints and key questions are given to show possible learning outcomes from the activities (and see Section 2.4 below).

2.3 Planning number experiences

The range of experiences for developing understanding of number will come from both planned activities and incidental interventions from adults in children's play. Experience of ordering, using number operations, larger numerals, recording and solving problems using number can occur in any nursery play environment and it is the skill of the adult to engage with the children and to help them to extend their language of number and their understanding through careful, sensitive questioning.

Setting up environments

Provide items for counting and sharing; materials which can be cut up, broken down or built up, such as dough; construction and block play, beads and laces; all can be used to encourage understanding of number concepts.

Numerals

Displays in the nursery should include numerals, both small numbers to ten and examples of larger numbers, such as telephone numbers, number plates on trucks and push-along toys. If magnetic numerals are available, children can use these to make their own recording, perhaps to show a telephone number (real or imaginary), to show prices in the café or hairdressers, or to put them in order. A large number line, with tactile numerals, will encourage the development of mathematical talk about numbers.

Number games

Number dice, as well as spotty dice, should be available for board and other games. Simple matching materials, such as snap cards which have quantities and snap cards

Table 2.1 Concept map for number

Key concept	Vocabulary	Examples of activities	Assessment checkpoints	Key questions
Begin to use the vocabulary of ordering	Counting numbers; one, more/fewer, first, second, third . . .; the same number as, as many as, more/most, bigger/biggest, fewer/fewest, smaller/smallest, less/least, compare, order, size	Running a race; who came first, second . . .; put picture cards in quantity order	• Orders quantities • Uses vocabulary of order to describe position	• Who has more/most . . .? • What would you rather have: two cakes or four cakes? Why?
Know that N+1 is one more than N and N−1 is one fewer than N	Counting numbers	Counting how many and one more; beads on lace; food onto a plate	• Knows how many for one more/fewer	• How many are there? (add/subtract one) Now how many are there?
Develop strategies such as finger counting, mental imagery, for addition and subtraction of small quantities	Counting numbers; next, before, more, fewer, add, take away, left	Hiding pennies in a money box/play people in the bus; put in two more/take two away; how many now	• Adds and subtracts small unseen quantities with reasonable accuracy	• I put three pennies in the money box, and now two more. How many are there? How do you know? • There are five people on the bus. I take out two. How many are left? How do you know?
Begin to relate addition to combining two groups of objects, and subtraction to 'taking away'.	Counting numbers; add, take away, leave, and, makes	Combining groups to find the total of: farm animals; cars; play people; threaded beads . . . Taking away from groups of things: crockery and cutlery in the home area; bricks	• Adds and subtracts using materials with reasonable accuracy	• There are some blue and red bricks here. Can you find a way of giving me seven bricks? How many red/blue are there? Can you find another way of doing this? You have six bricks. If I took three how many would you have? How did you work it out?
Begin to make reasonable estimates of small quantities	Counting numbers; how many, guess, estimate, nearly, close to, about the same as, just over, just under, too many, too few, enough, not enough	Farm animals in fields/shells in box; estimate then count to check	• Estimates small quantities with reasonable accuracy • Subitises for small quantities	• How many do you think there are? How did you work that out?
Recognise and use appropriate vocabulary to describe zero, both cardinal and ordinal aspects	Zero, none, nothing, all gone . . .	Putting out/putting away materials; running cars down a ramp; number rhymes and songs which count down to zero	• Uses vocabulary of zero in context • Knows when there is nothing left • Counts down to zero	• How many are there? • If I put them all away, how many would there be on the table?

Table 2.1 (continued)

Make fair shares of a quantity	Counting numbers; same, more, fewer, different, nearly	Sharing at snack time; sharing out playing cards, dominoes, fairly	• Shares a quantity into equal groups • Recognises when a sharing is unfair	• Share these between us; how many do you have? How many do I have? Is that fair? • Now share these between the three dolls . . .
Use vocabulary of division and fractions	Share, fair, same, different, nearly, half	Putting the same number of dolls into each pram; two play people into each room in the house; cutting paper/clay into two equal pieces	• Shares a quantity into equal groups • Recognises when a sharing is unfair • Cuts a whole into two similar (equal) pieces	• Share these between us; how many do you have? How many do I have? Is that fair? • Now share these between the three dolls . . . • How could you make this into two halves?
Name some larger numbers	Counting numbers beyond ten	Telephone, car, house numbers; counting rhymes, songs and stories with larger numbers	• Names larger numbers in context	• What is your house number? • Where can you find big numbers? • How do you know that these are big numbers?
Recognise contexts where larger numbers are used	Counting numbers; hundreds, lots	Shopping; prices; clock numerals; clothes sizes; shoe sizes	• Names larger numbers in context	• How much is that? • What time is it? How do you know that?
Make a record of numbers, using a pictographic, iconic or symbolic response	Counting numbers	Drawing pictures to show how many children; making tallies to show how many birds at the birdtable; writing numerals in the sand/on paper; making plasticine numerals	• Records to show how many with reasonable accuracy • Uses pictures, tallies or numerals to record quantities	• How many are there? • (Of numerals) what number is that? • Can you find me the number card to show how many there are?
Name some numerals and order them	Counting numbers	Recognising clock numerals; reading prices/telephone/car numbers; reading the numbers on a large number line; putting the numbers in number order	• Reads some numerals accurately	• What number is that? • Can you put these number cards in order for me? • What comes next? • What is between . . . and . . .? • How do you know?
Use developing mathematical ideas and methods to solve practical problems	Counting numbers; add, take away, share, What could we try next? How did you work it out?	Finding the same number in different contexts; totalling how many beads there are; working out the cost of buying items in the shop	• Uses number-based strategies to solve problems	• How many do you think there are? • How do you know that? • How did you work it out? • What could we try next?

Figure 2.7 There are many puzzles available which help children to read numerals

with numerals, so that children can match the quantity with the numeral, will help with numeral recognition and give practice in counting. Dot or picture dominoes can be matched for a given total, such as five or six.

Recording

To encourage recording, put a simple calculator, paper and pencils, and money in the role-play areas, such as the home area, café, shop and hospital. Children will enjoy writing shopping lists, recording how much money they spend or keeping a tally of how many drinks they serve. They may draw pictures or use tallies, rather than write numerals as their record. The calculator will be familiar to children as they will have seen it in use at home and in shops and they will include its use in their play. Numeral apparatus – such as magnetic, wooden or plastic numerals – should be available for children to use for recording.

Books, rhymes and songs

Books which include pictures for counting or ordering or where there is an increase or decrease of items on each page, and books which show numerals, should be clearly displayed in the book area. There are many number action rhymes which count up or down, or those that refer to a particular quantity such as 'Five little ducks that I once knew', and these can be used during circle time.

Number operations

Providing materials which can be shared, such as dough food in the home area, can offer experiences of sharing, addition and subtraction. Similarly, through planned activities such as cooking children can be encouraged to use their number skills.

Adult intervention in children's play

As was stated in Chapter 1, the skill of the adult worker in the nursery is recognising when it is appropriate to intervene in children's play. The intervention needs to extend the children's understanding, through careful discussion and questioning, encouraging children to use the number language that they have developed so far, and helping them to become familiar with new concepts and related vocabulary. The intervention must be supportive of what the children are doing. The following are everyday examples of events in the nursery:

- Ying Sum put three dolls into the aeroplane. She said 'One more, now there are four!' The nursery nurse asked 'And one more? Now how many?' 'Five!'
- Jamie and Peter, who had been working quietly at building trucks using a construction kit, had started to argue about how many wheels each child had. An adult intervened: 'Can you share the wheels between you?' Peter replied 'No. Jamie got four and I only got three. That's not fair.' The adult suggested that there should be another wheel in the box. They looked. Jamie said 'That's it. Now we can have the same. Four each.'
- On the table in front of the four children was a plate of orange segments. The adult asked 'Are there enough for us all to have one? How can we find out?' Emma suggested 'One each; one for you and one for you . . . and there's one left over. We've all got two.'
- Two children and an adult were walking to the local supermarket to buy some flour. Erin said 'That's the same as my house.' She pointed to a '34' on a house door. The adult asked 'What number do you live at?' 'It's a three and a four,' replied Sam. 'I live at thirty-four not three and four,' said Erin.
- The nursery 'shoe shop' had a shop assistant and a customer. The customer asked 'Please can I have some size 5 shoes.' The shop assistant went to the boxes and came back with a pair of high-heeled shoes. 'They're too big; I'll have size 4.' When the customer was satisfied the shop assistant 'wrote' a bill and said 'Two pounds please.'

Problem-solving strategies for number

Within children's play there will be opportunities for the adult to ask questions which help the children to use their number skills in order to solve problems. Questions that encourage problem-solving skills (Clarke and Atkinson, 1996) to develop include:

- What if there was one more/fewer?
- How many more is that?
- How can we give everyone the same?

Other questions can encourage evaluation of the project, such as:

- Can you find another way?
- I don't know if that would work. Let's find out.
- (To another child in the group) What do you think?

Focused activities

The following activities show the range of experiences that can be achieved through carefully planned focused activities for number. Such planning will enable the key concepts as outlined in Section 2.2 above to begin to develop.

Washing line game

An activity for a group of five children:

- *Purpose:*   to develop the language of ordering.
- *Materials:* washing line, pegs, cards with pictures on from one to five or more items, cards with numerals 1 to 5, or beyond.
- *Language:*   number words, one more than, one fewer than, before, after, next, first, last . . .

How to begin

Each child takes a picture card. They decide the cardinal value of it. They take turns to peg their card onto the washing line:

- Let's peg the cards on in order. Which one comes first?
- Which card comes after three?
- Which one comes next?

When all the cards are in order, ask the children to collect a particular card:

- Jasmin, will you take the card before three?
- John, will you take the one after four?

When they are confident with picture cards, the activity can be repeated with larger quantities. Where children are beginning to recognise numerals, numeral cards instead of picture cards can be used.

Baking

An activity for four children:

- *Purpose:*   to use the language of division and fractions.
- *Materials:* ingredients for making cakes; scales, bowls, spoons, bun tins.
- *Language:*   share, fair, the same, more, less, fewer, number words . . .

How to begin

When the cake mixture is ready to be divided into the bun tins ask:

- How many bun tins do you think we can fill?
- Will there be enough for us all to have a cake?
- How many do you think we can each have?

The children share the cake mixture out, and then discuss what they have done.

- Does each cake have the same amount of mix?
- How many cakes will there be?
- How many people can have cakes?
- If we eat all the cakes how many can we have each?

As the children answer the questions, there will be opportunities to observe the strategies they use to count and to share.

When the cakes are cooked and cool, they can be decorated. Children can decide how many sweets will be placed on each cake. When it is time to eat the cakes discussion can include:

- Choose a cake each.
- Jack, how many sweets are there on your cake?
- Who has more sweets on their cake than Jack?
- If you eat two cakes how many sweets will you eat?

Five button snowmen (Figure 2.8)
An activity for a group of four to six children:

Figure 2.8 Children can use a prepared snowman, with a waistcoat already drawn, or can draw their own

- *Purpose:* to explore different combinations to five.
- *Materials:* large snowman outline for each child, five identical buttons for each child, glue.
- *Language:* counting numbers, add, and, makes, altogether . . .

How to begin

Explain to the children that they have five buttons to put on the snowman's waistcoat. They decide how to place them. They might put two one side and three the other. As they try different combinations ask:

- You have put one that side. How many will go over there?
- How many over here? So how many more do you have? Count on from here, three . . .

The children can try different combinations, including zero and five. Either each child decides upon their preferred number combination and when ready sticks the buttons on, or the children agree that each snowman will be different, so that the finished snowmen show the combinations 5,0; 4,1; 3,2. The completed snowmen can be used as part of a snow scene.

This activity can be repeated for other quantities, perhaps using other shapes which can be partitioned, such as ladybirds or fish.

Involving adult helpers in the planned activities

Where number experiences have been planned, either through materials in the environments or through focused activities, all adults should be aware of the questions that can be asked to encourage the children to use number language. During the planning sessions, the adults agree on the range of language that might be appropriate and include it on their planning sheet for the week. Number language should be used consistently and correctly. For example, when referring to a numerical quantity, use few or fewer, not less, which refers to a measurement, such as 'There is less water in this jar'. Opportunities for children to record numbers during the week will occur incidentally. Adults can encourage children to write and to read back their recording, whether pictures, tallies or symbols have been used. With experience, children will realise that $1+N=N+1$. Adults can look for opportunities where this can occur, suggesting to children that they count the larger amount first, then one more.

Number activities for nursery environments (Table 2.2)

The following suggestions show the range of opportunities for developing number skills which can be planned, either through placing materials in an environment and encouraging children in their use of them to explore the language and actions of using number or by using these suggestions as a basis for planned, focused activities.

2.4 Assessment

Regular observations of children's use of number will identify their current knowledge and skills. Use the assessment checkpoints and key questions in Table 2.1 to help with assessment. The questions include both closed and open types. Observations, with evidence of the child's behaviour to support their understanding, can be recorded. Where evidence of achievement in a standard form is required, the

Table 2.2 Number activities for nursery environments

Environment	Concept/skill	Context
circle time	<ul><li>ordering</li><li>naming larger numbers</li></ul>	<ul><li>people maths with numeral cards: who should stand between one and three? next number after two?</li><li>discussing house numbers, ages of older siblings, bus numbers</li><li>songs and rhymes: singing number rhymes with larger numbers</li></ul>
daily routines	<ul><li>estimating how many</li><li>making fair shares</li><li>recognising some numerals</li></ul>	<ul><li>snack time: are there enough biscuits for everyone?</li><li>snack time: sharing out orange segments; does everyone have the same amount?</li><li>recognising numerals on a display: 4 can play in the sand</li></ul>
art and craft areas	<ul><li>making fair shares</li><li>using fraction language</li><li>recording numbers</li></ul>	<ul><li>sharing out some sequins for collage: does everyone have the same amount?</li><li>clay: cutting the sausage in half</li><li>painting flowers: painting a numeral to show how many flowers</li></ul>
table top games and collections	<ul><li>ordering</li><li>estimating how many</li><li>naming numerals</li></ul>	<ul><li>card games: ordering numeral cards, quantity cards</li><li>dominoes: estimating how many spots/pictures</li><li>numerals: reading numbers on dice/cards</li></ul>
sand and water	<ul><li>using number language including zero</li></ul>	<ul><li>emptying sand: counting how many cupfuls; using language of zero for nothing left</li></ul>
construction	<ul><li>counting one more/fewer</li></ul>	<ul><li>block play: how many? and one more/fewer?</li></ul>
role play	<ul><li>adding and subtracting</li><li>using larger numbers</li><li>using fraction language</li></ul>	<ul><li>home area: two dolls and teddy in the cot: how many altogether? Teddy out of cot: now how many?</li><li>telephone: dialling telephone numbers</li><li>shop prices: how much does it cost?</li><li>sharing out the food: half each</li></ul>
miniworlds	<ul><li>adding and subtracting small quantities</li></ul>	<ul><li>marina: how many sailboats? and one more/fewer?</li><li>garage: putting some cars by the petrol pumps; and one more/fewer?</li></ul>
outside play	<ul><li>counting one more/fewer</li></ul>	<ul><li>playing skittles: how many have you knocked down? and one more?</li><li>climbing frame: how many at the top? Jamie has come down, how many now?</li></ul>
pets	<ul><li>making fair shares</li></ul>	<ul><li>feeding the rabbits: put the lettuce in the bowls; give them the same amount</li></ul>

observational evidence can be supported by a note of the assessment checkpoint, with date and comment attached to show when the evidence of achievement was noted.

Regular observations will show whether children can:

- recognise that a quantity is larger/smaller than another;
- combine two small sets and say how many;
- take away a small quantity and say how much is left;
- make fair shares;
- use appropriate mathematical language for addition, subtraction and division;
- begin to recognise and name numerals;
- record using a recognisable system (pictures, tallies, symbols).

Some children may also begin to recognise how many more/fewer one set is than another.

Children respond well to questions such as:

- There are some blue and red bricks here. Can you find a way of giving me seven bricks? Can you find another way?

especially where they have been encouraged to respond using the mathematical vocabulary that they hear the adults using. Gradually they begin to respond in sentences and this should be encouraged.

What three and four year olds find more difficult are questions which ask 'How do you know?' such as:

- You have six bricks. If I took three how many would you have? How did you work this out?

Here the children tend not to respond to the second part of the question. PGCE students trialled some of the key questions in 2001 and discovered that young children did not cope well with this sort of question. However, with practice, and with examples of how they might answer given by adults, they do begin to answer the 'How do you know?' type of question in a satisfactory way.

Possible errors in using number

Those errors listed in Section 1.6, which refer to possible errors in counting, will also apply to the concepts and skills discussed in this chapter, because they, too, rely upon sound counting skills. Another source of error is from the concept of zero. This can be confusing as 'nothing' cannot be counted. Children will benefit from discussing what 'nothing' means in different contexts.

2.5 Working in partnership with parents and carers

There are many number-based activities which may already be used at home. Where the purpose of an activity is clear to parents and carers they will be encouraged to use carefully selected number vocabulary, as well as to become more aware of opportunities which involve number in normal, everyday life.

Activities at home for developing understanding of number

These activities do not require any special equipment, as they make use of everyday items in the home.

Recognising numerals

- *In the home:* numerals on television, the telephone number, setting the video, looking at the clock, reading picture counting books together.
- *In the street:* finding a 4, a 3 . . . on car number plates, on price labels in shop windows, looking for bus numbers.
- *In shops:* looking at prices, finding the same and different prices.

Using numbers

- *Ordering:* dot-to-dot puzzles; sewing cards.
- *Addition and subtraction:* at breakfast counting how many slices of toast each person eats, how many in total, how many have been eaten.
- *Division:* sharing out sweets so that everybody has the same; counting to check.

Number games

- *Playing cards:* placing in order, from 1 to 5, or beyond.
- *Picture cards:* finding cards which total three, four or five.
- *Dominoes:* playing fives, where the two touching numbers total five.
- *Board games and larger numbers:* snakes and ladders, with numerals to 100.

CHAPTER 3

Pattern

Recognising that a sequence of objects makes a pattern, explaining why, being able to copy, extend and create a new pattern are early steps towards an appreciation of spatial patterns, and number patterns and relationships, and towards an appreciation of the power of algebra. That the study of algebra can be exciting was recognised in the proposals for the Mathematics National Curriculum (DES, 1988):

> Mathematics is not only taught because it is useful. It should also be a source of delight and wonder, offering pupils intellectual excitement, for example, in the discovery of relationships, the pursuit of rigour and the achievement of elegant solutions.

By the end of the reception stage in school, or for a four year old in a nursery class, the children are expected to be able to:

- Talk about, recognize and recreate simple patterns.

(DfEE, 2000)

What is pattern?

Pattern can be described as a systematic arrangement of numbers or shapes which follows a given rule. Some shape patterns have repeated sequences of shapes and each sequence is usually in the same order (Figure 3.1). Other shape patterns can show growing patterns of shapes. In number patterns there is a definite relationship between the elements of the sequence, such as 0, 2, 4, 6, 8, 10, 12, 14 . . .

Figure 3.1 This is a linear shape pattern. The sequence of square, circle and triangle can be repeated as many times as wished

3.1 How children develop understanding about pattern: research findings

Piaget and Inhelder (1967) studied children's acquisition of understanding about pattern. They described understanding of pattern as topological in nature. (See Chapter 4 for discussion of development of topology in young children.) To make sense of pattern, children need to develop ideas of 'betweenness', that is, that in a sequence of three, the middle one is between the first and the last (Figure 3.2).

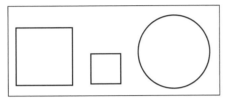

Figure 3.2 In order to describe a sequence, it is necessary to be able to describe what comes between two items. Here the small square is between the large square and the circle

Babies

Piaget found that young babies begin to recognise patterns very early in their life. At first, they recognise spatial succession; for example, when they observe two, separate items ranged one before the other. They will see items which are fixed in order, such as the rungs of their cot, or the arrangement of furniture in their bedroom. They will also recognise habitual movements, such as the door opening followed by their mother entering the room, and then being fed.

Two to three years of age

At this age Piaget and Inhelder (1967) found that children were unable to reproduce a sequence of items in a particular order. For example, they may well choose beads which correspond to those that have been threaded, but cannot copy the threaded sequence. They do not yet understand proximity (nearness) and so do not observe the order of the objects.

Three to five years of age

Between three and four years of age, Piaget and Inhelder (1967) found that children were beginning to be able to copy objects in an order. For example, they might peg clothes on a washing line to match the order of the clothes already there, or thread some more beads to match the order of those already threaded. Piaget observed that children would not always reproduce the same order: for example, when copying a bead sequence of red, blue, green, yellow, their order might be green, yellow, red, blue. At three years of age they are beginning to get some proximities right (the closeness), but not all of them.

At four years of age, children can understand order if they can keep a constant check on it. For linear sequences the copy needs to be directly under the original so that they can make constant comparisons and copy the sequence in the same order (Figure 3.3). For circular order, children are still unable to maintain the correct sequence but will choose the correct items for the sequence.

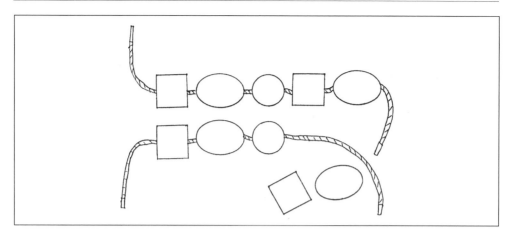

Figure 3.3 The original threaded lace is placed above the one to be made so that children can make a direct comparison as they work

By the age of five, most children are still unable to reverse the order of items, such as reversing red, blue, green, yellow beads to yellow, green, blue, red. It is not until children are five to six years old that most of them will be able to place a pair of shoes together correctly for left–right orientation. Many reception teachers will attest to how children can put on their shoes, but will randomly select a shoe for each foot, so that there is an even chance of putting the correct shoe onto their right foot.

3.2 Making patterns and key concepts

The immediate implications from Piaget and Inhelder's (1967) findings may well be to question whether it is appropriate to include pattern work for pre-school children. Althouse (1994) describes how, when making body movement patterns, most four year olds could describe a three-word body sequence, such as touching head–eyes–shoulders, head–eyes–shoulders . . .; and she found that some five year olds could teach others five- and six-word body sequences. She also noted that when children 'understood "what comes next" in relationship to "what came before" they had no difficulty understanding and making patterns'. To recognise a pattern children must be able to identify similarities and differences and order – that is, what came before, what comes after. They will need to use mathematical language of pattern, such as same, different, before, after, next, copy, repeat . . . The development of ideas about similarities and differences is complementary to developing understanding about numbers and their value, and shapes and their properties. In this book, the view is taken that children can be encouraged to develop understanding about what makes a pattern, how to copy patterns and how to make their own as these experiences can not only enhance understanding in other areas of mathematics, but also enhance children's experiences of art, music, physical movement. Understanding about pattern involves recognising rules, such as repeating bands of colours on wallpaper where red stripes always follow white ones.

How their understanding of pattern concepts can be enhanced by an appropriate nursery curriculum is the focus of this section. The development of pattern concepts is considered under the following headings:

- describing an order
- describing and making line patterns
- copying a sequence
- creating a sequence
- creating a pattern
- recognising cyclic patterns.

The activities through which children explore concepts of pattern are likely to encompass more than one aspect of pattern. Many children will copy a sequence and then repeat it, or make their own repeating motif, whilst for example using mosaic tiles. For each of the experiences listed above, a wider focus than mathematics will be taken, as, at this stage, children's own explorations of sequence and pattern will take them into art, music and movement experiences as well as more mathematical ones of shape and number patterns. The concepts associated with order, sequence and pattern are valid in all these areas.

Describing an order

Children will experience order in many different contexts, such as putting dolls onto chairs in order of size, threading beads red, blue, red, blue, or making a printing pattern using alternately a sponge and a cork. It is through the discussion with an adult that children will begin to understand the order within their pattern. Asking questions such as 'What came first?' and 'What comes next?' will encourage children to note the order of items in a sequence and extend this to their pattern. As they become confident in making repeating patterns with two items this can be extended to three.

Such orders can have various characteristics:

- *Colour.* Observations of strings of beads with alternating colours will encourage children to note the order of the colours. When children are painting, they can make striped designs, for example, red then blue then green. When children have undertaken a minibeast hunt they may well have found striped caterpillars. Or on a visit to the zoo they may see a zebra with alternating stripes of black and white. For all of these it is the opportunity to discuss what is seen, to describe the order of colours, which helps children to understand regular, repeating sequences which make a pattern.
- *Shape.* When making a string of beads, children can be encouraged to alternate two shapes of beads. In sand play, they might use two different containers to make sand pies, and alternate these. When building with blocks or other construction

kits, children can make repeating patterns with the blocks, noting which shapes they use and checking that the order is consistent (Figure 3.4). Gura (1992) shows that children will repeat a particular construction, perhaps making a pattern with the blocks, and that when the routine is well established they will collect the blocks needed to make their construction before they begin. This suggests that they are using order and repetition to build their pattern.

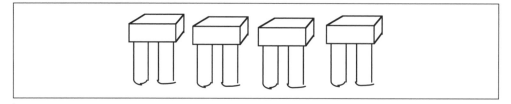

Figure 3.4 Pattern made with cuboid and cylindrical blocks

Similarly, observing patterns in fences, railings and in wire netting (Figure 3.5), where the order of shapes gives rise to the pattern, will help children to see that items are ordered.

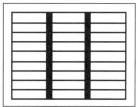

Figure 3.5 There are patterns in the horizontal and vertical struts of the fence

- *Size.* Comparing items for size, for example in the role play of the story of The Three Bears, encourages children to compare size, and to order by size. They can make dough shapes of the bears, and order these by size. Again, it is the use of language which will help children to recognise the order. When making dough shapes, children can make repeats of longer, shorter, longer, shorter . . . worms and describe their position within the order. When using percussion instruments children can be encouraged to make repeated orders of loud and soft sounds. If they listen to another's pattern of sounds, and observe the strong followed by gentler movement to produce the sound, they will experience the rhythm of making such an ordered sequence of sound.
- *Texture.* Some of the textured velvety fabrics or textured wallpapers have distinct patterns made by alternating raised and flat areas. When using pieces of fabric, perhaps to wrap dolls, children can be encouraged to observe the fabric and describe what they can see and feel, noting the alternating contrasting sections.
- *Position.* Children's own movements, where they are encouraged to make high then low movements, can become an ordered pattern, such as 'Stretch up high; crouch down low; stretch up high; crouch down low'. They can experience

making these ordered movements, and observe each other. Similarly, when using musical instruments, they can make alternating high and low sounds, again listening to others and experiencing the repeated nature of movements and sounds, in order.

- *Quantity.* Orders using quantity may occur during children's play. They might make a tower of four bricks followed by one of three bricks, then one of four bricks and so on. Here there are opportunities for comparing quantities, that three is one fewer than four, and of identifying that three follows four, follows three. Similarly, in movement, children can make two jumps and a step, two jumps and a step, and so on. By observing one another they can see and describe the movements and compare the quantities.

Sometimes children will use a combination of the above in order to make a sequence or pattern. Catherine (five years) and Rebecca (four years seven months) were threading beads to make dolls' necklaces:

Catherine: Now the red then the blue. Over and over.
Rebecca: Mine's different. Pink and silver. Pretty!
Catherine: Look. Red and round, blue and long!

Catherine had realised that she was sorting the beads by more than just colour criteria in order to make a consistent pattern.

Describing and making line patterns

In Chapter 4, painting, drawing, printing and sewing as means of exploring lines are considered in a 'shape' context. When considering patterns, line patterns, with their repeats of shapes such as curves, zigzags, straight, loops, thick and thin lines, offer excellent opportunities to consider what changes and how, and to observe the repeating nature of the pattern. When sewing, children come to realise that there is a rhythm to this activity which is repeated with the needle, to make a row of stitches: up and along, down and along, up and along, down and along . . . At first, children will explore lines in a free form way, producing 'scribbles' when finger painting, covering the paper without taking account of repeatable actions in their drawing. This becomes modified as they begin to note the regularity in line patterns.

- *Free form designs and patterns.* Children will enjoy using finger paints to make their own designs. They can use sponges to make prints, and feathers, toothbrushes, combs . . . in order to make random designs on paper. They can be encouraged to describe the design they have made, to hear and use language such as straight, round, curved. When using items such as combs, the print effect will have a sequence of lines in parallel to each other. Scrapers with teeth (the type which come with tubs of tile adhesive) can be used to make swirling, parallel lines (Figure 3.6).
- *Printing with objects* (Figure 3.7). When making prints with potatoes, cotton reels, foam shapes, leaves . . . at first these will be randomly placed on the paper.

Figure 3.6 Swirly patterns can be made with a scraper pulled through finger paint

Children can be encouraged to print in a straight line, placing one foam-shape print after the other. If two colours are used, then they can make repeats of colour in a straight line.

Figure 3.7 Printing with foam shapes or potato cuts can be used to make ABAB repeat patterns

- *Line patterns* (Figure 3.8). Using pencils, crayons or paint, children can produce straight lines, thick and thin, zigzags, loops, or curves. As they make their repeats they should be encouraged to note the repeated movements which they make. Observing another making these patterns will help them to associate the repeated movements with the pattern. Similarly, such patterns can be made in dry or wet sand using spades, sticks or pencils of different widths so that they can compare their patterns. Alternatively, children can spread finger paint and make line patterns in it. Where children have access to computer drawing software, they can make interesting effects with repeated lines.

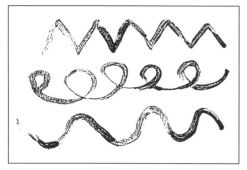

Figure 3.8 Paint can be used to produce interesting line patterns

- *Direction* (Figures 3.9–3.11). Line patterns which change direction, such as those which can be made on sewing cards, encourage children to recognise the in-and-out, up-and-down patterns. Similarly, computer drawing software will allow them to explore the movements where there is a change of direction.

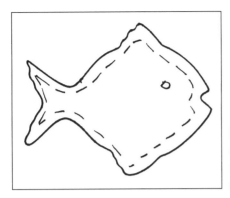

Figure 3.9 Using sewing cards gives experience of the up, down, up, down movement as well as seeing the pattern of the stitches.

Figure 3.10 Blot and fold patterns can produce interesting line effects which show the effect of reflections

Tomas and Fiona (both aged four years) worked with an adult in the nursery. They were making marble prints, running marbles around a tray with splodges of paint in the bottom, then taking an impression of the design onto a sheet of clean paper. They were totally engrossed in what they were doing and did not speak as they worked. When they had finished their prints, the adult asked what they could see.

Tomas: Lots of lines. Look. Long ones.
Fiona: Lots of colours. Look, red and blue and green.
Adult: When they're dry, shall we mount these to go on the pattern display?

Copying a sequence

Copying a sequence helps children to recognise the order in which the elements of the sequence are placed. To make an accurate copy they will need to recognise what comes first, what comes next and what is last. Where the sequence is repeated, they will, through careful questioning and discussion with an adult, come to realise that the elements of the sequence are always repeated in the same order, such as making a line of toy vehicles which repeats red bus, blue car, yellow lorry, red bus . . .

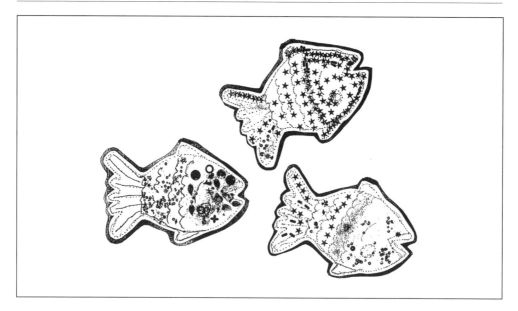

Figure 3.11 Using collage, in this case gummed shapes and sequins, can also produce some interesting line effects

Where children are encouraged to discuss the sequence, they may begin at one end, describe the sequence and then consider it from the other end. Is it the same? Why? If not, can they explain why not?

- *Making a direct copy.* From Piaget and Inhelder's work (1967) it might be supposed that young children will find copying sequences too difficult. However, in most nursery classes children will be found copying sequences, of movements, music, words and rhymes, bead patterns, and so on. These are activities well within the grasp of most four year olds. Through careful observation, and with the original sequence directly in front of them, children will copy a simple pegboard sequence, or make a tower of bricks which matches the one their friend has made. It has been noted (Gura, 1992) that in their block play children will repeat, day after day, a particular structure, making the structure from memory. This ability to repeat the same structure demonstrates that making copies is well within their capabilities. Children will copy a simple clapping rhythm, perhaps to represent their name (Figure 3.12).
- *Making repeats.* In learning to copy a simple sequence, children may well copy it over and over again, forming a repeating pattern. This can be seen where children thread beads to make a necklace and copy their original design, such as blue, green, blue, green . . . until the necklace is long enough. Similar repeats can be observed in other activities, such as repeating a sequence of taps on a drum or on some chime bars. Davies (1995) describes how a three year old developed her own game, moving under a clothes rail which had bottom and top rails and uprights. She repeated her movements, saying 'under and over' again and again, copying her own sequence of movements and words.

Figure 3.12 Clapping patterns

Creating a sequence

Children will create their own sequence, of movement, music, threaded necklace, or structures. In a reception class in the Netherlands, the teacher had set up a black tent, which was very dark inside. On a table inside the tent were some beads, laces, sequins, shiny buttons, shiny papers and fabrics, glue and paper, and mirrors. There were dressing-up clothes made from shiny fabrics. A jewellery box contained bracelets, brooches, earrings and rings, all made from shiny materials. Children went into the tent with a torch. They threaded beads to make a necklace, or stuck shiny papers onto plain paper, in each case to make a sequence. Some children dressed up in the shiny clothes, then put on the necklace that they had made or chosen from the jewellery box. The effects that they produced were lovely, and they were excited to observe shiny things in the dark, with just a torch for light. Those who made necklaces threaded, unthreaded and rethreaded the beads and sequins to get the effect that most pleased them. They discussed what they had produced, talking about colour, shape and size, as well as their preferences and dislikes.

Creating a sequence which is pleasing to the child will involve discussions of likes and dislikes, favourite colours and shapes. Where children work cooperatively, sharing materials, they can be encouraged to compare what they have created, looking for similarities and differences.

During a movement session, the reception class children were asked to copy a simple dance sequence of stretch up tall, curl up small, jump up and stand still. The teacher noted that some produced the movement sequence without error, but that the younger children, who were just four years old, did not seem to remember the sequence and repeated the stretch and curl, or the jump and stand still. She asked some of the children who found this difficult to work with a partner and copy their movements whilst she spoke the movements in sequence. Quickly all the children produced the sequence of movements, in order.

Creating a pattern

To create a mathematical pattern, children will need to understand about repeats. They may have observed patterns on fabrics or wallpapers and noted how these repeat. They may have noticed when singing that some songs repeat lines, or have a repeating rhythm of clapping to accompany them. Such patterns are linear patterns, where the pattern repeats can continue to infinity.

- *Creating a sequence and copying it.* Such a pattern can be very simple, an ABAB pattern, with alternating colours, shapes or sizes. These can be created by the children using, for example, pegs and boards, beads and laces, construction kits, play people, or items in the home area. Some children may make patterns where they make an 'answering phrase' such as an ascending then descending staircase of bricks, or printing lines, each one wider than the previous one (Figure 3.13). All of these are patterns in their own right, and children should be encouraged to talk about what they have made, and discuss how their pattern could be improved.

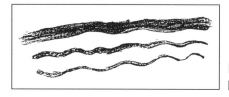

Figure 3.13 Thin, thicker and thick lines can be painted to make interesting line patterns

- *Creating a growing pattern* (Figure 3.14). This can be a simple staircase pattern, made with rods or bricks, or a pattern where one item grows with each repeat.

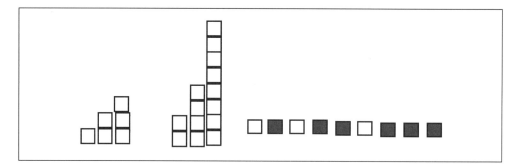

Figure 3.14 Growing patterns

Recognising cyclic patterns (Figure 3.15)

Cyclic patterns are patterns which join to make a seamless, continuous pattern. For example, a threaded bead pattern, with red, green, blue, red, green, blue, when looped to make a necklace, will continue the sequence, in order, and without a break.

Cyclic patterns can be made from materials, such as making decorated paper bangles or crowns, or sitting toys around a table, where the toys alternate doll, teddy, doll, teddy . . . Time patterns can be cyclic, such as night following day, the order of meals, or the life cycle of plants and minibeasts. Young children may recognise both as patterns.

- *Making cyclic patterns with apparatus.* Making a pattern which repeats in a cycle can be quite difficult, as children need to ensure that the repeats of the sequence will fit into the space available for the cycle. For example, if a child puts out five chairs around a table and chooses teddies and dolls to sit in an alternating ABAB

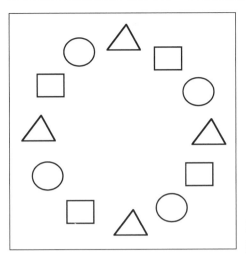

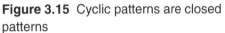

Figure 3.15 Cyclic patterns are closed patterns

pattern, then it is not possible to finish the cycle as two toys of the same type will sit next to each other. Discussion with children will help them to identify where their pattern is 'wrong'. Their solution may be to put an additional chair at the table between the two toys which are the same. It is more likely that at this stage, children will complete a cyclic pattern by addition, such as adding more beads to a necklace until the pattern closes.

- *Recognising aspects of time which are cyclic.* This is another aspect of cyclic pattern which children may wish to explore. For example, they will begin to recognise that there are regular repeating aspects of their lives, such as night follows day follows night follows day . . . There will be regular routines during the time at nursery, such as the order of events with perhaps story time following snack time and going to the toilet then washing their hands. Those children with younger siblings may recognise the regular order of events with the baby, such as feeding, changing the nappy, baby sleeping . . . For all of these, discussion is key, as it helps children to recognise the order of events and that they repeat in a regular pattern. Children may recognise the repeating nature of the days of the week, or of the analogue clock, with its rotating hour and minute hands. See Chapter 5 for further discussion of Time.
- *Recognising life cycles as cyclic.* This is much more difficult and will only be touched upon at nursery. However, children who have pets at home may have experienced birth, growth, ageing, death . . . as a cycle which is repeated with pets with short life spans such as hamsters or gerbils. However, as one repeat of some of these cycles lasts for longer than the child's life to date, it is unreasonable to expect children to understand life cycles as cyclic pattern until they are older. Those who have a garden, or help to grow plants in the nursery garden, may experience the repeating cycle of the plants.

Problem-solving

Possibilities for problem-solving with pattern will arise as part of children's everyday activities. For example, where new curtains are to be made for the home area, children could decide to decorate them with a printed pattern. They can be encouraged to develop their problem-solving skills by:

- describing the pattern they wish to make;
- choosing the materials for printing, refining their choice as they work;
- carrying out their plan, with adult intervention to discuss how closely their plan fits their original planning, and the reasons for changes made;
- reviewing the finished pattern, describing its features, and checking that the sequences repeat;
- using appropriately the language of pattern in their discussions.

The need to solve problems will arise during children's chosen activities. When decorating a paper hat to make a pattern around the crown, children can be encouraged to consider how they will ensure that the pattern is continuous around the crown. This can be quite difficult to ensure as it will involve deciding how many pattern repeats will fit and spacing the pieces around the crown. The adult's role is crucial, ensuring that sensitive questioning and suggestions extend the learning opportunities and encourage children to set and solve problems for themselves.

Concept map (Table 3.1)

This shows the concepts outlined above in matrix form together with examples of vocabulary which can be developed. Example activities are shown so that the map can be used as a basis for planning. Assessment checkpoints and key questions are given to show possible learning outcomes from the activities (and see Section 3.4).

3.3 Planning pattern experiences

It is important for all adults working in the nursery to be aware of possibilities for developing children's understanding of pattern and to have appropriate subject knowledge and understanding of the concepts and vocabulary associated with pattern. A child threading beads to make a bangle can be encouraged to make a repeating pattern of colour or shape, or a combination of both, or perhaps to make a growing pattern of bricks, using one, then two, then three, in a row. The adult's role in identifying possibilities and intervening in the child's play in a sensitive manner is most important, as this can produce opportunities to introduce and extend children's understanding of the concepts and vocabulary associated with pattern. Many of the experiences that children will have will come from their own choice, such as working with the blocks, threading beads, printing, and using sewing cards. All of these experiences offer opportunities for children's awareness of pattern concepts and language to be enhanced.

Focused activities

Planned activities for developing pattern concepts will often include opportunities to develop several concepts, rather than just concentrating upon one aspect. The

Table 3.1 Concept map for pattern

Key concept	Vocabulary	Examples of activities	Assessment checkpoints	Key questions
Describe an order	Before, after, follow, next, start, finish, between	Using beads and laces, pegs and boards, mosaic tiles, construction kits describing an order by size, shape, texture, position, quantity	• Identifies positions within the order, e.g. before, after • Uses vocabulary of order appropriately	• What comes next/before/after? How do you know? • Can you make a new pattern using these . . .?
Describe and make line patterns	Lines, loops, straight, thin, thick, zigzags, , curves, out, in, up, down . . .	Printing, drawing, painting, imprinting in sand; making patterns and designs and describing the pattern	• Describes the line shape • Uses a range of lines to make patterns and designs	• Which shapes have you used? • Can you make a different pattern using these lines?
Copy a sequence	Copy, same, different, start, finish, repeat, again . . .	Copying a pattern sequence of threaded beads, bricks in a tower, movements, rhythms; describing the sequence; checking that the copy is the same	• Copies a sequence accurately • Identifies any differences	• Are these patterns the same? • (Of a sequence with one piece different): Is this the same? What is different? Can you make these the same? How did you do that?
Create a sequence	Start, finish, middle, between, next, before . . .	Sewing cards and laces, printing, imprints in plasticine, imprints in sand; deciding the order and describing position	• Uses imagination to make a sequence • Describes the order	• Can you make a different pattern using the same pieces? • How is it different? • What will come next/between . . .?
Create a pattern	Start, finish, middle, between, next, before, copy, same, different . . .	Threading beads in a regular pattern, building a block pattern; deciding upon the sequence; checking that the sequence repeats to make a pattern	• Copies a sequence to make a pattern • Creates a sequence and copies it correctly to make a repeating pattern	• Can you make me a pattern where the second bead is red? Is there another way of doing that? • What will come next in your pattern?
Recognise cyclic patterns	Before, after, next, between . . .	Making decorated crowns, bracelets, putting toys in a circle; describing the repeating pattern, e.g. ABAB; talking about time patterns: day/night; order of events of the day . . .	• Describes a cyclic pattern • Finishes a cyclic pattern keeping repeats correct • Uses vocabulary of position and cyclic time	• What comes next? • Can you finish the pattern? • Tell me about your day: what did you do next? . . . and next?
Use developing mathematical ideas and methods to solve practical problems	Pattern, puzzle, what could we try next? How did you work it out?	Plan the pattern, choose materials, carry out the task and review it	• Makes patterns and describes them using appropriate vocabulary	• What other patterns could you make? • What other materials could you use to make that pattern? • How did you work it out? • What could we try next?

following activities demonstrate both planning for a range of concepts, and activities which concentrate upon just one concept.

Pegboard patterns (Figure 3.16)

An activity for a group of four children:

- *Purpose:* to copy a sequence and describe its order.
- *Materials:* pegs and boards, with a simple colour sequence of pegs at the top of each board.
- *Language:* copy, same, different, start, finish, before, after, follow, next, between . . .

How to begin

Each child has a board with the same colour sequence of pegs at the top.

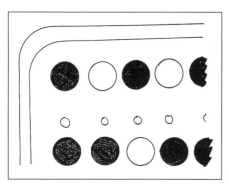

Figure 3.16 Pegboard sequence

The children describe the position of the pegs in the sequence:

The red peg is before the blue peg.
The green peg is after the blue peg.
The first peg is red.
It finishes with the green peg.

When they have described the positions of the pegs, they copy the pattern on the next line of the pegboard.

Choose one child's pegboard and ask them all to shut their eyes. Alter the position of one of the pegs in the original sequence and ask the children to open their eyes. Ask:

- What has changed?
- Which peg is first now?
- How do we make Sally's pattern the same as this one?
- Which peg is between the blue and the green?

The children can choose three or four pegs and make their own order. Ask them to describe the position of the pegs.

Line patterns

An activity for four children:

- *Purpose:* to make and describe line patterns.
- *Materials:* examples of line patterns from wallpaper or fabric samples, paint, paper, brushes of different thicknesses, pieces of stiff card, feathers, old toothbrushes, comb . . .
- *Language:* straight, line, thick, thin, loop, curve, zigzag, in, out, up, down . . .

How to begin

Show the children some examples of line patterns, and encourage them to use appropriate vocabulary to describe what they see. Ask them to find specific examples of line pattern such as:

thick straight line
thin curved line
wavy
zigzag

and to describe the pattern.

- It's a zigzag. It goes back and forward over and over.
- It's wavy, just like the sea.
- This one is curly.

Ask the children to make a design on their paper, using different sorts of line patterns. They may choose from the painting implements; alternatively, they might use their fingers to make the patterns. When the designs are finished, ask:

- What shape is this? Can you find me another one like it?
- Which lines have curves?
- Which lines have straight pieces?

The children can experiment with various thicknesses of paintbrushes to explore the different line patterns they can make.

Snack time patterns

An activity for four children. Where the use of foodstuffs as part of an activity is not appropriate, small items such as buttons can be used instead:

- *Purpose:* to create a sequence then a repeating pattern.
- *Materials:* dried fruit such as raisins, apricots, sultanas.
- *Language:* start, finish, next, before, copy, same, different . . .

How to begin

Ask the children to choose three pieces of dried fruit and put them in an order. Ask questions to encourage them to describe their order:

- Which piece is first?
- What is between your apricot and raisin?

When the children can repeat their order in words, ask them to copy their order, and again, and again, to make a repeating pattern. Ask them to check that the order is always the same:

- Sam, does the raisin always come before the apricot?
- Patty, what comes after your sultana?
- Noreen, is this the same as this (pointing to sections of the pattern)?

When the children understand that patterns can be made from repeating sequences, ask them to use their fruits to make a different pattern. Also, make patterns with mistakes in the repeats for the children to find and correct. The pieces of fruit can be eaten during snack time.

Patterns in the sand
An activity for three or four children:

- *Purpose:* to create patterns.
- *Materials:* sand, sand tools, such as rakes, moulds, buckets, pebbles, feathers, shells, flags . . .
- *Language:* start, finish, middle, next, before, copy, same, different . . .

How to begin
Ask the children to choose from the tools to help them to make their own repeating pattern in the sand. When they have finished, ask them to describe their pattern:

- Mine has lines, then a pebble, then lines, then a pebble.
- I've got two shells, then a sand pie.
- First there's a shell, then a pebble, then a feather. I put a line all the way along. Then it's the same.

Ask the children to change their pattern. Look to see if they remember to change the repeat.

Instead of using the large sand tray, these patterns can be made in shallow plastic trays so that children make individual patterns. These can be put on show as part of a pattern display.

People patterns
An activity for everyone during circle time:

- *Purpose:* to create a growing pattern.
- *Materials:* the children, dressing-up clothes such as hats and scarves.
- *Language:* start, finish, next, more, between, copy . . .

How to begin

The children will need to sit in a straight line so that they all observe the activity from the same viewpoint.

Ask one child to put on a hat and another to put on a scarf. They stand in a line in front of the others. The other children say the sequence that they see: hat, scarf.

Ask another child to come out, give him a hat to wear and to stand in line, then the next child to put on a scarf and stand in line. Ask the children still sitting what comes next, a hat or a scarf.

This can be repeated until everyone is in the line, wearing either a hat or a scarf. The children can take turns in saying what they are wearing, along the line, so that they will hear the repeating pattern of the words 'hat, scarf, hat, scarf . . . '

Ask everyone to sit down, then choose four children to stand in a line, choosing their own order, such as hat, hat, scarf, scarf. Ask those still sitting down what they think should come next, and next, and so on, building the repeats of the pattern until everyone is in line. Again, ask the children to say in turn what they are wearing, so that all hear the pattern.

Ask some of the children to stand in your chosen order, such as: sit, stand, sit . . . Continue the pattern, making a deliberate mistake. Ask the children as each child joins the line:

● Is this right? What comes next?

Check that they identify the mistake and can tell why it is wrong.

This activity can be repeated with children standing or sitting in different positions, such as:

● sit, stand, sit, stand, sit . . .
● hands up, hands up, hands down, hands up, hands up, hands down (Figure 3.17) . . .
● legs astride, kneel, sit, legs astride, kneel, sit . . .

The pattern repeats can become more complex if this is appropriate and can include growing and shrinking patterns, such as:

● stand, sit, stand, stand, sit, stand, stand, stand, sit . . .
● child standing in a hoop, two children in hoop, three children in hoop, four children in hoop, three children in hoop, two children in hoop, one child in hoop.

Movement patterns

An activity for everyone during a movement session:

● *Purpose:* to copy and create a movement sequence.
● *Materials:* the children.
● *Language:* first, next, begin, start, finish . . .

How to begin

The children line up one behind the other, with, if possible, adults in the line to help. Explain that the game is a follow my leader one, and that they copy the

Figure 3.17 Hands up, hands down, hands up, hands down . . .

actions of the leader (an adult). The actions must be a repeated sequence of three or four movements, such as step, step, step, jump. The children follow the leader around the room, repeating the actions. It is helpful if the leader chants the actions so that the children hear and see the sequence.

When the children have learnt the pattern, individuals can demonstrate to others and they can say the repeating sequence.

Now give other simple movement sequences for the children to copy on their own, such as:

- hands up, hands down, crouch down, hands up, hands down, crouch down . . .
- step, step, clap, clap, step, step, clap, clap . . .

This can be extended by individuals making up their own simple sequence for others to copy.

Musical patterns

An activity for everyone during circle time:

- *Purpose:*   to copy and continue a pattern.
- *Materials:*   percussion instruments.
- *Language:*   start, finish, copy, same, different . . .

How to begin

Choose a familiar song that the children enjoy singing. Decide upon a simple, repetitive rhythm to accompany the song and while the children sing the song clap or tap the rhythm on a percussion instrument. Now ask the children to clap the rhythm as they sing. Ask:

- How does the rhythm start?
- Who can clap it for me?
- Does this sound right? (and clap it, making a mistake)

When they are confident at this, choose some children to use percussion instruments instead of clapping.

Musical tunes

An activity for four children:

- *Purpose:*   to create a repeating pattern.
- *Materials:*   chime bars which play some notes from the pentatonic scale, items to record the music, such as coloured cubes, coloured crayons, paper, cassette recorder.
- *Language:*   start, finish, copy, same, different . . .

The pentatonic scale (Figure 3.18) is very useful as in whatever order the notes of the scale are played it always produces a pleasant sound.

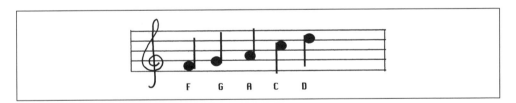

Figure 3.18 Pentatonic scale

How to begin

Start with just two chime bars each. The children create a simple sound sequence which they copy to make a simple repeating pattern. When they are confident with this, they can use another chime bar to make their musical pattern more complex. Record their patterns using the cassette recorder and play this back. Ask:

- How might you change your pattern?
- What comes first now?

When they are satisfied with their pattern, record it again and play it back.

Encourage the children to explore ways of recording their repeating pattern. They could use coloured cubes to represent the order of the chime bar notes, or make coloured marks on paper. When they have recorded, ask them to play their pattern using their invented musical notation. Then play back the original from the taped version. Ask:

- Are they the same?
- What have you changed?

When they are satisfied with their musical pattern and their recording, the taped version and the cube or coloured crayon recording can be placed on the music table for others to enjoy.

Growing and shrinking number patterns from songs

An activity for everyone during circle time:

- *Purpose:* to make shrinking patterns.
- *Materials:* nursery number rhymes which count forwards such as 'Peter hammers with one hammer'; 'This old man'; 'One elephant went out to play' or which count backwards, such as 'Five little buns in the baker's shop'; 'Ten fat sausages'; 'Ten in the bed'.
- *Language:* count back, how many, start, finish, number names in order forwards and backwards . . .

How to begin

Decide whether to use songs which count forwards or count backwards. Sing the song with the children and ask at the end of the first verse 'How many more . . .?' or 'How many fewer . . .?'

Many children find songs with actions help them to remember the number patterns, for example putting up or down the required number of fingers. Other songs involve one more child standing in front each time, such as in 'One elephant went out to play.'

These nursery rhymes can be used to encourage children to recognise the growing or shrinking pattern of the numbers and to relate these to 'how many'.

Cyclic patterns

An activity for four children:

- *Purpose:* to recognise cyclic patterns.
- *Materials:* large, medium and small Compare Bears and 2D shapes cut from card, such as squares, circles, hexagons.
- *Language:* before, after, next, between . . .

How to begin

Ask children to count out four large blue and four small green Compare Bears. They put the bears around the circle (or 'table'), in an ABAB repeating pattern. Ask them to say the pattern: large blue bear, small green bear, large blue bear, small green bear. . . . If the children do not realise for themselves, point out that the pattern does not stop, but continues around the circle (Figure 3.19).

This time, using two of blue, green, yellow and red large Compare Bears, ask the children to arrange the bears in a repeating pattern around the circular table. Ask, using the square:

- How can we put these bears at this table?

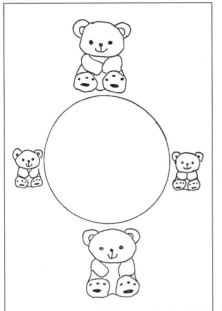

Figure 3.19 Cyclic pattern

Encourage the children to place the bears in a regular pattern around the table, for example, placing two at each side of the square. This can be repeated using six bears, three blue and three red, to be placed around the hexagon table, and then using twelve bears, three of each colour, in order to encourage copy and repeat patterns.

Instead of using Compare Bears, this activity can use dolls, teddies, chairs and tables. Alternatively the children can be given specific features such as wearing a hat or a scarf, and make themselves into cyclic patterns.

Cyclic patterns of time

An activity for a group of four to six children:

- *Purpose:*   to encourage recognition of the cyclic nature of time.
- *Materials:*   photographs of routine events in the nursery, or time sequence cards.
- *Language:*   before, after, next, between . . .

How to begin

Show a small selection of the photographs, out of time order. Ask:

- What comes first?
- What comes next?

and so on until the photographs have been ordered. Each child takes a card and then lines up in time sequence order, deciding:

- What is first? Is this what happens first thing in the morning?
- What comes between snack time and going home?
- What is last? Why is that?

On another occasion, place the photographs in a nonsensical order. Ask the children if the order is correct and encourage them to change the order, one photograph at a time, and explain why they have made the changes.

Involving adult helpers in the planned activities

Pattern, in its broadest sense, occurs all around us and there will be many incidental opportunities to discuss pattern with children. A child wearing a new jumper, with a Fair Isle or Jacquard pattern, can be encouraged to describe the pattern, noting the pattern repeats, the colours and the shapes. This may prove to be a useful example of a cyclic pattern, as it may continue unbroken around the jumper. Language associated with pattern concepts is also language used in everyday life. This language should be used correctly and in appropriate contexts. The language to be developed can be included on the weekly planning sheet and during planning sessions. Work with patterns will produce some attractive results which the children will appreciate being displayed for others to see. Where there is space, a 'Pattern table' can be set up, with examples of patterns which children have made.

Where there are adults from other cultures in the nursery, they can be encouraged to show examples of patterns from their cultures and traditions and help children to make their own representations. For example, children will admire a beautiful sari, with a border repeat pattern; they will enjoy looking at examples of Islamic patterns. Similarly, special events, such as a child's birthday, can offer opportunities to explore and create patterns, such as making a repeating pattern on a cake, making the same design on each biscuit, or making and decorating with a repeating pattern a piñata for a birthday party.

Special festivals are opportunities for adults in the nursery to bring to bear the specialised knowledge of how these are celebrated. The following are just a few of the festivals from religions other than Christianity that might be considered.

- *Divali:* a Hindu festival, which means 'row of lights'. Clay lamps are used to provide light, and these can be made from clay or dough. Women make chalk patterns called rangoli outside their houses.
- *Raksha Bandhan:* a Hindu festival, which means 'protection' and is for brothers and sisters. Girls make their brothers a bangle, usually red-coloured, called a rakhi and the brothers give their sisters a present.
- *Eid:* an Islamic festival, which marks the end of the month of fasting, Ramadan. People give Eid cards, which are sometimes decorated with Islamic patterns.

For special interests, it may be possible to invite people in from the community, perhaps to show the children a craft which involves the use of pattern. These might include spinning and weaving, knitting, or crochet work.

Pattern activities for nursery environments (Table 3.2)

Table 3.2 Pattern activities for nursery environments

Environment	Concept/skill	Context
Circle time	• copy a sequence • copy a pattern • create a sequence or pattern • recognise a cyclic pattern	• singing songs with repeats • playing percussion accompaniments • composing rhythms and tunes and recording them for playback • reciting order of the days of the week
Art and craft areas	• copy a sequence • create line patterns • create a sequence • create a pattern • describe sequence or pattern	• making sequences and patterns by: painting, printing, drawing, cutting and sticking • starting sequences for others to copy/continue
Table top games and collections	• copy a sequence • create line patterns • create a sequence • create a pattern • describe sequence or pattern	• using collections to make sequences and patterns: pegs and pegboards, beads and laces, buttons, sorting toys, mosaic tiles, Fuzzy Felt, magnetic tiles . . .
Sand play	• create sequence or pattern • describe sequence or pattern	• making ABAB patterns of sand pies in damp sand • using sticks, rakes, combs, shells, feathers, imprints, to make sequences and patterns
Construction	• copy a sequence • create line patterns • create a sequence • create a pattern • describe sequence or pattern	• choosing construction pieces to copy a sequence or pattern • making ABAB patterns with construction kit pieces • making structures with a pattern in their design
Block play	• copy a sequence • create line patterns • create a sequence • create a pattern • describe sequence or pattern	• choosing blocks to copy a sequence or pattern • making a sequence or pattern using at least two different types of block • making structures with a pattern in their design
Role play	• describe sequence or pattern • complete a cyclic pattern	• describing fabrics, wallpapers in the home area • dressing up: choosing a necklace with a complete cyclic pattern
Miniworlds	• describe sequence or pattern • create a sequence or pattern	• putting cars in straight lines of alternating red/blue/red/blue . . . • lining up the animals to go into the farm: cow then pig then horse, cow then pig then horse . . .
Outside play	• recognise a cyclic pattern	• helping to grow plants in the garden: observe the cycle of planting, growing, dying, planting . . .
Cooking	• create line patterns	• icing cakes and biscuits with lines
Information technology	• copy a sequence • create line patterns • create a sequence • create a pattern • describe sequence or pattern	• using art software to copy sequences and patterns • using art software to create sequences and patterns

3.4 Assessment

Regular observations of individual children, noting their use of language and how they copy, continue and create patterns, will give useful evidence of what children can do and what they understand, and identify aspects of counting where children lack confidence. Use the assessment checkpoints and key questions in Table 3.1 to help with assessment. The questions include both closed (how many?) and open (how do you know?) types. Observations, with evidence of the child's behaviour to support their understanding, can be recorded. Where evidence of achievement in a standard form is required, the observational evidence can be supported by a note of the assessment checkpoint, with date and comment attached to show when the evidence of achievement was noted. Regular observations will show whether a child can:

- Describe an order, using appropriate language of position.
- Describe and make line patterns, using language of size, shape, position and movement, and of thickness.
- Copy a sequence, making an exact copy.
- Create a sequence, discussing the start, position of elements, and its finish.
- Create a pattern, by repeating a sequence and checking that the pattern repeats are correct, or by making a growing or shrinking pattern.
- Recognise cyclic patterns, and state the position of elements in the pattern.

Opportunities for assessment will occur through discussion with children about their pattern making, encouraging them to use the language of position correctly. Outcomes from children's activities, such as printed patterns and threaded bead patterns, can be used as part of the assessment process, especially where this is accompanied by the children's comments about their work.

There will be incidental opportunities for assessment as well as those arising from planned activities.

Children respond well to questions such as:

- Can you make a new pattern using these . . .?

especially where they have been encouraged to respond using the mathematical vocabulary that they hear the adults using. Gradually they begin to respond in sentences and this should be encouraged. Indeed, when PGCE students in 2001 trialled these questions for the author the children responded eagerly to this question, and although they found it difficult to respond verbally, they showed with the pattern pieces that they understood what to do and could respond appropriately.

What three and four year olds find more difficult are questions which ask 'How do you know?' such as:

- What comes next/before/after? How do you know?

Here the children tend not to respond. The PGCE students discovered that young children did not cope well with this sort of question. However, with practice, and with examples of how they might answer given by adults, they do begin to answer the 'How do you know?' type of question in a satisfactory way.

Possible errors in concepts of pattern

As with concepts of shape and space (see Chapter 4) children's understanding of pattern will be limited by their awareness of topological concepts, particularly proximities. Possible errors may include:

- The inability to reproduce a sequence of items in a particular order. They may choose the correct items to copy the sequence, but then place them in a haphazard order. They do not yet understand proximity (nearness) and will identify the individual items but not their relative order. As the children mature they will begin to understand proximity and so both choose the correct items and put them in order.
- Inconsistency in copying a pattern. Children may copy some of the sequences correctly, but not do so consistently. This shows that they are beginning to understand proximities, but not with consistency.
- Inability to copy a sequence unless the original is directly above the copy. The children at this stage can only make direct comparisons. Where the sequence to be copied cannot be placed directly above the copy, the copying may well be inaccurate.
- Inability to copy a cyclic pattern while choosing the correct items for it. Again, this is the result of a lack of maturity, and as they begin to understand more about proximities, they will be able to copy a cyclic pattern. An example of this occurred in a reception class. It was nearly Christmas and the children were making and decorating party hats. Each child was asked to make a repeating pattern on their hat from coloured shapes. Whilst they produced a repeating pattern along the crown without help, they all needed adult intervention in order to achieve a pattern that was continuous around the crown, that is, a cyclic pattern.
- Ability to make a sequence, but not to reverse it, that is red, blue, green; green, blue, red. Children lack left–right coordination until they are about five to six years old. However, with adult help, and careful comparison of their pattern, and with a mirror to observe the reflection of the pattern, children's ability with reverse patterns will improve.

Where a child consistently confuses colours in patterns this may be due to colour blindness. If this is the case, then instead of making colour patterns the child can make patterns from shapes.

3.5 Working in partnership with parents and carers

At home, children will have real-life experiences of pattern. Whilst shopping for wallpaper or clothes children will see repeating patterns and hear these discussed, perhaps hearing language associated with pattern. They will see patterns in the environment, perhaps a repeating pattern of wall tiles or wrought-iron railings, or they may become aware of short life cycles, such as those of the butterfly or frog. These experiences, and those specifically designed for use at home, will provide an enriched pattern experience to encourage children to recognise, copy and create patterns.

Activities at home for developing understanding of pattern

These activities do not require any special equipment as they make use of everyday items in the home.

Pattern walks
- *At the shops:* describing patterns on dress materials, packaging materials; observing tile patterns on walls and the ground.
- *Houses:* describing patterns in roof tiles, bricks, railings, fences, manhole covers, windows.
- *Going to the park:* observing and describing patterns in flowers, fir cones, birds' feathers.

Line patterns (Figure 3.20)
- *Cutting out:* making repeating patterns.
- *Making line patterns in dough:* straight, curved, zigzag, wavy, wiggly lines.
- *Drawing and painting:* making line patterns, using different thicknesses of crayons or paintbrushes.

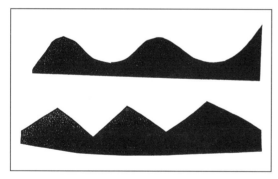

Figure 3.20 Cutting out line patterns

Patterns in the home
- *Tiles:* describing repeating patterns in floor and wall tiles.
- *Wallpaper:* finding the pattern repeats; looking for similar patterns, same shapes, different colours; finding line patterns.
- *Clothing:* finding cyclic patterns on socks and jumpers; finding patterns of colour, shape, line or a combination.
- *Wrapping paper:* describing the patterns; finding the repeats.
- *Packaging:* describing patterns on cans, boxes and bags.
- *Using mirrors:* observing patterns, then observing them in a mirror and describing what has changed.

Making patterns

- *Using construction kits:* making staircase patterns, making towers with alternating coloured pieces blue, red, blue, red . . .
- *Using small items:* lines of animals, buttons, conkers, acorns or marbles, to show ABAB, or ABCABC patterns.
- *Cyclic patterns:* using Fuzzy Felts; mosaic tiles.
- *Cooking:* making icing patterns on cakes and biscuits; putting food on the plate to make a repeating pattern such as carrot, peas, carrot, peas.

Time patterns

- *Ordering events when cooking:* making sandwiches and describing the order.
- *Ordering events during the day:* describing what has been done in order.
- *Growth:* planting seeds, caring for the young plants, harvesting the crop.
- *Days of the week:* repeating the sequence of the days.

Movement and dance patterns

- *Dancing:* moving to a repeated sequence of movements.
- *Music:* making repeating rhythmic sequences using home made instruments such as cans or boxes with dried peas or rice inside, tapping with spoons, scraping wood on sandpaper.

Nursery rhymes and stories

- *Counting forwards:* On the first day of Christmas; One man went to mow; One, two, buckle my shoe.
- *Counting backwards:* Five currant buns in the baker's shop; Ten fat sausages; Ten green bottles; Ten in the bed.
- *New and favourite stories:* re-telling the story, remembering the order of events.

CHAPTER 4
Shape and Space

The expections of the Early Learning Goals are that by the end of the reception stage in school, or for a four year old in a nursery class, the children are expected to be able to:

- Use language such as 'circle' or 'bigger' to describe the shape and size of solids and flat shapes.

(DfEE, 2000)

4.1 How children learn about shape and space: research findings

For many adults there is no relationship between the study of shape and space, or geometry, and of number. However, like arithmetic, shape and space concepts conform to rules of equivalence (similarity) and transformation (difference or change) and it is this conformity which ensures the linking of number and shape and space into part of the subject 'mathematics'.

(Haylock and Cockburn, 1989)

What is the study of shape and space, or geometry? John Mason (1991) defined geometry as '. . . the dynamics of the mind; what is "seen"'. He described geometry as being apparently in the physical world, but actually in the mind, and recommended that it is taught so that children have a means of organising their sense of shape and space.

Much of the research into how young children develop concepts of shape and space refers back to Piaget (1965; Piaget and Inhelder 1967) and his research, which showed that early concept formation was topological. (Topology is nicknamed 'rubber geometry' because of the way in which shapes can be transformed by squeezing and stretching one into another.) There has been little contemporary research. The Russian researcher Leushina believed that children oriented themselves in space as the basis of a personal reference system using their own body, firstly towards themselves and later towards an object, then later still being able to consider relationships between objects and other people. He considered that children used topology as well as 2D and 3D geometric relationships. Russian researchers came to the view that concepts of space begin with 2D shape, then 3D and finally topology as a final or global applications stage (Thorpe, 1995).

Australian research (Thorpe, 1995), which looked at pre-school children's understanding of spatial concepts, found that children did not explore many topological notions, but used topology as the basis of their 2D and 3D exploration in play, such as block play. She found that children rarely used language to reinforce notions of position. She concluded that children used notions of topology first, then position, then 3D and 2D concepts. Her research supported Piaget's conclusions. She noted that children learnt through interacting with their environment through play and that sensitive adult intervention was very important to encourage concept and language development.

The view that is taken in this book supports that of Piaget, confirmed by Thorpe (1995), that children begin with topological notions of spatial concepts. The Piagetian view is that very young children's first concepts of shape and space are topological, that is, they perceive objects in terms of:

- proximity or nearby-ness of objects;
- separation or identifying an object from others nearby;
- order or spatial succession, such as the door opening and someone coming into the room;
- enclosure or surrounding;
- continuity of lines and surfaces.

Research by Clements *et al.* (1999) showed that whilst young children use the visual matching to identify shapes they also begin to recognise components of shapes and simple properties so that by the time that they are six they become quite sophisticated in their ability to sort and classify 2D shapes.

4.2 Young children's understanding of shape and space

The main references for this section are Hohmann *et al.* (1978), Piaget and Inhelder (1967) and Piaget *et al.* (1960). Where other research has been consulted, this is referenced in the text.

Birth to two years

At first, the world must appear very disorganised. People come and go out of the line of vision. Shapes appear not to be rigid, but often change, so that the mother is seen from different views, such as far away, near, side view, front view. Babies show awareness of only those objects that they can see. If a toy falls out of sight, they seem to regard it as no longer existing and will turn to another object. As babies learn to sit up, then crawl, they become more mobile and can search for objects which are not within their immediate vision. As they learn to stand, then walk, they learn that they are located in space and test this out by moving themselves and their toys.

They discover that objects change position, for example when the drinking cup is dropped from the high chair, and will repeat this over and over again, each time observing the effect. They enjoy searching for hidden items, such as opening their parent's closed hand to see what is hidden inside. They make chance discoveries, such as poking fingers through holes, posting shapes into the posting box by random selection of shape and hole, but gradually refining the process as they recognise which shape matches which hole – and then testing this by trying the wrong shape to the wrong hole – and often laughing whilst carrying this out. Straight lines are perceived very early in life.

By the time they are two years old, they can find toys which have rolled out of sight, showing that they can now represent space mentally, such as in searching for a brick that has slid under a sofa (Copeland, 1979; Hohmann *et al.* 1978). They are beginning to discriminate between straight and curved, but not a square from a rectangle nor a circle from an ellipse. Their drawings are unrecognisable scribbles. Their early understandings of shape and space are formed from visual and tactile exploration (Figure 4.1).

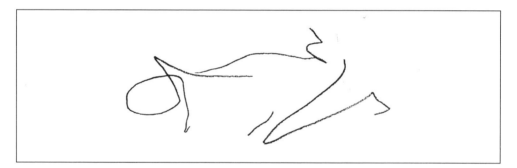

Figure 4.1 Drawing of a cat, by Sarah, one year nine months

Three to five years

Soon children can distinguish between open and closed figures, but without discrimination of the properties of different closed figures. Their drawings at this stage are what Piaget described as 'synthetic incapacity', where the main part of the drawing is recognisable and will contain items that are misplaced. In a drawing of a man, for example, the mouth may be placed above the nose. Proximity is not adhered to in detail, but the elements are distinguishable from each other (separation). Items may be reversed or misplaced (order); eyes might be drawn outside the face (enclosure); and features may be juxtaposed (continuity). It is not until children are about seven years old that they draw figures using proportion, distance and perspective; until then they use topological characteristics.

If a three year old is asked to make a copy of a triangle, they may draw a circle. From the topological perspective, this is correct, as a triangle can be stretched and squeezed until it forms a circle. Both shapes have the same property of being closed, that is the drawing begins and ends at the same point (Copeland, 1979) (Figure 4.2). Open shapes such as crosses are more accurately drawn, but straight lines are unlikely to be straight.

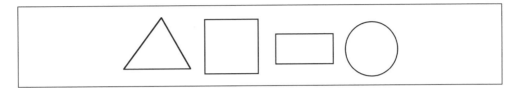

Figure 4.2 All these shapes are closed curves. They can be squeezed or transformed into each other

Research by Lovell (Bass, 1975) leaves open the question of whether children acquire topological concepts before Euclidean geometrical ones. Lovell found that young children found it easier to construct shapes using match sticks than to draw them. Similarly, Golomb (in Wales, 1990) found that children could model in clay items which they were unable to draw in recognisable form.

At about four or five years of age in their recognition of pictures and drawings, children will begin to differentiate 2D shapes, distinguishing curves from straight, but not usually triangles from squares. Few children will reach the stage of 'intellectual realism' in their drawings. This is where the child draws everything that can be seen. Proximities are correct, with, in a picture of a man, legs and arms attached to the trunk. Separation is clearer; interiors of figures may be shown such as food in the stomach (enclosure). Pictures are not yet structured in terms of perspective and general coordinates. They understand 'straight' and can envisage and make straight lines using objects when the background contains some examples, such as making a row of cubes in line with the edge of the table, but they find this impossible if there is no point of reference for 'straight line'. It is not normally until children are five or six years old that they can make a straight line with no point of reference for 'straight'. More recent research than Piaget (Borke, 1983), shows that children of three and four have some understanding of perspective when presented with situations which are familiar.

Three year olds begin to develop understanding of proximity (how close things are) and of separation (how far apart things are). They enjoy taking things apart and putting them back together, arranging and rearranging things in space. They may develop a schema (Gura, 1992), that is, a repeatable pattern of behaviour which is not tied to specific contexts, making enclosures with bricks, loops with string, drawing circles. They are beginning to describe where things are in space and the direction in which things are moving. They may confuse distance with effort, believing that going up the slide involves going further than sliding down. However, Piaget *et al.* (1960) noted that at this age they were beginning to develop a good sense of direction, but had difficulty with position, so that they confused 'in front' with 'behind' when they turned round, and similarly, 'left' with 'right'. They begin to understand spatial enclosure, discriminating between things with and without holes, and between a closed loop of string with something inside it and one with something outside it. They make their own enclosures and use language, for example 'inside' and 'outside', to describe position. They understand 'line' but find it difficult to make a straight line, either by drawing or by lining up objects such as cubes. Their lines are topological. They have no conception of perspective.

Between three and four years children begin to understand spatial enclosure. They can discriminate between objects with and without holes and between a closed loop of string with something inside it and another with something outside it. In their play, they make enclosures and use language such as 'inside' and 'outside' to describe what they are doing. They begin to use language of position, next, near, on top of . . . to describe where either they or their play materials are. They explore their environment by climbing, swinging and balancing on climbing frames, pushing and pulling trucks, stacking blocks to make stable and unstable piles, and twisting to take lids off jars. They are becoming agile and aware of what their bodies can do. They learn where items such as toys and books are kept in the home and the nursery and can take responsibility for getting these out and putting them away again. They are more aware of the space around them, and of position and movement to reach things.

They will be becoming aware of relative position, so that they may view a chair a few metres away as being close to them, but if an object is placed between themselves and the chair they will no longer view the chair as close and their perception will be that the chair is now farther away.

At this age they may not believe that objects which have been moved to a different position are still the same objects and take up the same amount of space. They may not believe that blocks built into a tower, then taken down and made into a pattern on the floor, are still the same blocks; they note the before and after arrangements, not the process of changing blocks from one arrangement to another.

When making clay models, children cannot imagine what shape will be left after they make a cut through a section. This is so, even when a cut will make a section with identical features to the original shape, such as a transverse section of a cylinder (Figure 4.3). Their drawings show views of intact exteriors and imaginary sections.

Drawings of solid shapes are not 3D representations but are of a face of the shape until children are five or six years old, for example a square for a cube or rectangle for a cuboid, a circle or triangle for a cone. Their 2D shape drawings, once distinguishable as triangle, circle, square, will not discriminate different types of these shapes, such as right angled from scalene triangle.

4.3 Spatial experiences and key concepts

What children may be able to do by the time they start mainstream school is outlined above in Section 4.1. How their understanding of spatial concepts can be enhanced by an appropriate nursery curriculum is the focus of this section. The development of spatial concepts is considered under the following headings:

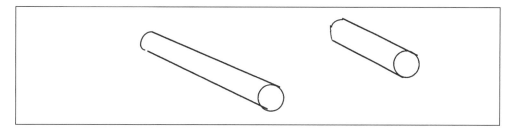

Figure 4.3 A transverse cut of a cylinder leaves two cylinders

- describing natural and manufactured shapes;
- constructing and deconstructing shapes;
- simple properties of 3D shapes;
- exploring lines;
- simple properties of 2D shapes;
- reflection and symmetry;
- position and movement;
- interpreting pictorial representations of spatial relationships.

However, these concepts overlap each other and the same experience can be used to encourage development of understanding across a range of concepts, such as, whilst making models, describing junk packaging, the shapes, what the packaging originally contained, and how the boxes best fit together.

Describing natural and manufactured shapes

Children will have explored their environment through touch, taste, smell, sight and sound of what is around them. Through adult intervention in their play and through focused activities they can be encouraged to use new language to describe shapes, using the language of classification. They can investigate natural objects, such as leaves, bark, stones, shells, flowers, seeds and minibeasts, as well as manufactured items. They will enjoy making their own objects from clay and junk materials and can be encouraged to describe those, choosing from these classifications:

- *Texture.* Children respond to touching an object by describing what they feel, whether it is smooth, soft, hard, rough, bumpy, sharp, has points . . . This may link with scientific exploration, especially when children are observing natural items which they have collected, such as crinkly autumn leaves, soft petals on flowers, or sticky clay.
- *Colour.* Children will be beginning to use colour names to describe objects. They can sort by colour for both natural and manufactured items. They may separate toy cars by colour, putting red ones on one road and blue ones on a different one on the floor plan. Sorting autumn leaves by colour, they can find reds, yellows and browns of differing hues.
- *Features.* Children can make collections by what is common, and can be encouraged to use shape properties such as things with holes in them (airflow balls, colanders,

lacing board, slotted spoon . . .), rings (hoops, quoits, bracelets, necklaces . . .), things with lids (saucepan, box, jar . . .).

Other features which children will encounter include:
- shapes with 'insides': boxes, tins, bottles, shells . . .
- twists and turns: telephone cable, rope, liquorice or barley sticks, some shells, screws, pasta spirals . . .
- knots: tied shoe laces, parcels tied with string, fastenings on dolls clothes . . .
- flat surfaces: cube dice, bricks, boxes . . .
- curved surfaces: balls, spoon bowls, wheels . . .
- solid shapes: bricks, blocks, table tops, dolls . . .

- *Differences.* When sorting, children may find items which do not belong in a set. They can be encouraged to find the odd-one-out from collections. Using a feely box with a collection inside, children can find the piece of velvet amongst the rougher fabrics, the ball amongst the bricks, the doll's cup amongst the plates . . . They can make their own collections of similar items and then add something which does not belong. It is the discussion of why something does not belong, using shape and other classifying language such as colour, texture or size, which will help children to develop the concept of difference as well as the concept of 'the same' or 'similar' as they identify the common and different features.
- *Size.* As they compare two or more items children can be encouraged to describe the differences using size, such as larger and smaller ball, longer and shorter plank, thicker and thinner twig . . . Comparisons of size are considered in detail in Chapter 5.

When children are investigating they will probably use a mixture of the above means of classifying shapes in order to describe what they have found. Tammy was four years old and had picked up a conker.

Tammy: What's this?
Adult: It's called a conker. Where did you find it?
Tammy: There. (Points to under a chestnut tree.)
Adult: Look up. Can you see those prickly balls? Those are conker cases. Let's pick one. (Pulls a conker case from a lower branch.)
Tammy: It hurts!
Adult: Yes. It's a special case to keep the seed safe. There should be a conker inside. Shall we look? (The adult opens the case to show the conker.) What does your conker look like?
Tammy: My conker is bigger . . . brown . . .
Adult: Yes and it's round . . . smooth . . . hard. And the case is green with prickles on it. Feel inside the case.
Tammy: Lovely. Smooth.
Adult: Does your conker fit in this case?
Tammy: (Tries the case for her conker). Too big (referring to her conker).

Here Tammy uses colour, shape, size and texture to describe what she has found. She spent some more time that morning trying to find a container for her conker so that it was safe and returned to the adult later with a doll's teapot.

Tammy: Look. Fits.

Adult: I think there's some more room. How many conkers can you fit in there, Tammy?

Constructing and deconstructing shapes

As young children develop so they become increasingly aware of the spatial relationship of objects and that some things will come apart and can be fitted together again. They may use trial and error methods to find what fits, such as pushing a jigsaw piece around until it falls into place, as if by accident. They will fill jars with treasures, pour sand into buckets to make sand pies, and play with jigsaws. These are all examples of putting together or taking apart to explore how shapes fit and how new shapes can be made. Children will benefit from opportunities to explore:

- *Fitting shapes together.* They will put scissors in the scissors holder, felt pens in their box, stack rings on a post, nest beakers one inside the other, play with jigsaws, build with blocks and construction kits . . . Each of these activities gives opportunities for looking at fit, whether there are gaps and whether the pieces are in the correct place. They can describe the fit using language such as on top, underneath, next to . . . They can also talk about items which do not fit together and why this is so, which will encourage the development of their observation skills.
- *Taking shapes apart.* In many nursery settings children will have opportunities to build large constructions which they can climb inside, or make large models which can sit on and move. Through these activities they can explore how the pieces fit together and which pieces fit in particular places to make their model. They may take apart one model and make something different with it, so that they explore the range of shapes which can be made with the same pieces. Using questions such as 'How else can the pieces fit?' or 'Where will this one go?' children can be encouraged to build mental images of their models whilst they are being made, and of the likely finished product.

Rearranging and reshaping objects

When building models, children will frequently take them apart to make changes. Encouraging them to describe what they plan to do, are doing, or have done, will assist them to use mathematical language of shape and of position. Similarly, when making playdough models children will reshape their dough to change what they are making, so that a ball of dough becomes a snake or a cat.

- *Rearranging objects.* Children may move pieces in a construction to change its shape or its function. As they become more aware of how the pieces fit together they will begin to recognise whether or not a piece will fit in a different position. They may move objects such as doll's house furniture, changing its position.

They may build a high tower with blocks, then use the same blocks to rebuild into a wall. Describing these changes, using language of shape and position, will help children to build mental images of shapes and where they will fit, especially if questions of the 'what if . . . ' type are used.

- *Reshaping objects.* Changing the shape of dough models, folding pieces of paper or doll's clothes, stretching rubber bands, making and changing a necklace from poppet beads, are all examples of ways in which children can alter the shape of an object. They can be encouraged to try new changes, again by asking 'what if . . .?' questions. They can be encouraged to copy shapes, for example, when making a pot from dough, and to describe what they are doing.

These experiences encourage children to consider how shapes can be made and changed, where pieces can fit, and to use language of shape and position. They may begin to explore volume, particularly through activities such as making and reshaping a piece of dough into something new. They may make straight lines, curves, shapes with holes or insides, and change them so that they, or a toy, can fit inside the shape they have made.

Tim and Ben (four years five months) made a truck with the Quadra. When it was finished, they sat in it for a while, pretending that they were in an aeroplane. They discussed their model with an adult and both expressed interest in helicopters. With help, they made a top for their truck, with blades. Another adult asked about their work.

Tim: It's a big helicopter now. The top goes round and round.
Adult: How did you make it?
Tim: We made a car. It was boring.
Ben: We made a top for it. Sally (an adult) helped make the top.
Tim: Where we sit. It's the same.
Adult: Do you both fit in?
Ben: Yes and we're going to fly away.

Simple properties of 3D shapes

From experiences of sorting and classifying objects, fitting shapes together and taking them apart and rearranging and reshaping objects, children will have had opportunities to explore some of the properties of 3D shapes. From their experience of 3D objects, which can be handled, children can make observations which will help them to begin to understand about 2D shapes, for example, that the tin of baked beans has 'round' or circular end faces, that the tins can be stacked one on another if the 'round' faces are put together and that if they turn the tin on its side it will roll. They usually sort and classify according to shape before they use shape names. Adult intervention may well include the use of more formal language, which will help the child to begin to give a name to the concept of 'square' or 'circle'. Children may draw, paint or model flat shapes. They usually become adept at making circles; squares and triangles come later (Hohmann *et al.*, 1978). The learning of formal, geometrical names for shapes has usually been left until mainstream school; pre-fives can often recognise and name boxes, cones, cylinders (tins, cans) and pyramids.

Through experiences of working with shapes, and discussion, children will begin to recognise the following properties of shapes:

- *Face shapes* including curved, straight, flat, points and edges. These can be flat or curved. Some shapes have corners or points, for example cubes and cuboids, others do not, such as cylinders and spheres; the cone has both. Through finding shapes which fit particular criteria from a selection on display or from inside a feely box, they will develop the concepts of flat and curved, points, and edges.
- *Movement*, or rolling and sliding. Through throwing balls and quoits, and sliding toys down a ramp, children will have opportunities to explore properties of movement. Although in theory rounded shapes roll and shapes with flat faces slide, flat-faced shapes can be made to roll if the gradient of the slope is steep enough. This property can be explored through encouraging children to change the gradient of the slope until all the objects they are using will roll down the slope.
- *Arrangements*, through stacking 3D shapes and building strong structures (Figure 4.4). From choosing shapes to fit together to build a model, children will have discovered that flat faces fit together and form strong structures, that cylinders will only stack with circular faces together, and that some shapes are not suitable as building blocks, such as spheres, cones and pyramids.
- *Properties* of solidity and hollowness, exploring insides and outsides, and unfolding and folding nets of 3D shapes. These properties may be easier to explore as part of a focused activity, so that children are encouraged to discuss what they observe. Commercial packaging, such as sweet boxes and cereal boxes, will unfold if undone along the seams. Sweet packaging is particularly useful for this as it comes in so many different shapes and sizes. Children can take the boxes apart, fold them flat, look at the shapes of the flattened packet, then fold it up again. They may use construction kit pieces to make their own boxes and take them apart and put them together again.

Exploring lines

Painting, drawing, printing, and sewing with lacing cards, form part of the everyday activities from which children choose in the nursery. All of these offer opportunities for children to explore lines which are straight, curved, zigzag, loops, thick and thin. Making lines of different widths, and of various shapes, then discussing the shape, thickness and direction of the lines, will encourage development of the following concepts:

- *Line shape* which includes straight, curved, zigzag and loop. Using different printing materials will produce a variety of lines, such as straight with the edge of a piece of card, curved with string, zigzags and loops with felt pens, paint or crayons.
- *Thickness*, developing ideas of thick, thin, wide and narrow. Thick brushes will produce a different line from thin ones, and different again from a toothbrush or

Figure 4.4 Wooden blocks for building come in many shapes and sizes

nail brush. Printing with a feather can give a very thin line, or a thick one depending whether the fine edge or flat face of the feather is used.

- *Outlines*, developing the ideas of shape, turn, straight and bend. Tracing around the outer edge of a shape will encourage awareness of the shape enclosure. This can be achieved through tracing around shapes in the sand tray, using sewing cards, drawing around shapes, and printing with objects which will make a clear outline, such as the inside of a jam jar lid.
- *Direction*, including forward, backward, straight on, and turn. The language of movement can be developed through exploring lines. This can be achieved

through painting and printing, and also through the use of painting and drawing software, which enables children to produce different types of lines, a variety of shapes, with outlines or filled in. Most of this software has the facility to alter shapes, by stretching and turning. Programmable toys, such as PIP and Roamer, can be programmed by the children to explore movement. If a pen is attached to PIP or Roamer children can see the trail of the line of movement which is left and can re-program Roamer to move back along the same line or to make different line patterns. Similarly, children's own movements can be used to explore lines, through nursery action rhymes such as 'Farmer's in his den', or 'Looby Loo', or through moving on trucks and tricycles outside, in different directions and using straight, curved and zigzag movements.

In all of these experiences, it is the interaction between child and adult that enables the use of new language to develop. Children's schema for 'straight', 'curved' and so on, will develop through activities such as those suggested above, and through copying, repeating and devising their own patterns with lines and shapes. (See Chapter 3.)

Simple properties of 2D shapes

Making pictures with shape tiles, Fuzzy Felt, or magnetic tiles, are regular nursery activities. From a mathematical perspective, it should be recognised that children are working with 3D objects, not 2D, and recognising and, later, naming the surface of the object as circle, square . . . Children can describe the shapes which they have combined to make their picture, perhaps begin to name some of them, such as circle and square. Where children use shapes to make repeating patterns, printing with corks, sponges, feather . . . there are strong links between this work and pattern, in Chapter 3. Concepts to be developed here are:

- *Combining 2D shapes.* At first, children may use shape tiles which are recognisable as objects, such as Fuzzy Felt people and animals, flower heads, and pieces of fencing. They will enjoy combining different pieces to make recognisable pictures, putting wheels onto a car body outline, or making an owl, with ears and eyes. Mosaic tiles, which have mathematical shapes including circles, triangles, squares and rectangles, can be used to make patterns. Children may explore which shapes will fit together, leaving no gaps (beginnings of tessellation) and, through discussion, begin to name some of the shapes, particularly circle or 'round'. They may use these shapes in drawings, perhaps making a picture of a cat with a 'round' body, or the sun as a circle.
- *Sorting 2D shapes and naming them.* Choosing shape tiles for a picture offers opportunities for sorting and naming 2D shapes. Shapes used should include everyday shapes as well as mathematical ones. Children can sort stars, moons, animal templates, transport and house templates or sorting toys, so that they have experience of making a set with common features and the opportunity to discuss what is common, such as 'points' on stars, that the sun is 'round'.
- *Making patterns with 2D shapes.* (See Chapter 3.) Printing with bottle tops, corks, feathers, toothbrushes . . . gives children opportunities to explore the surface

shape of these objects. They can compare the cork with the print left by its circular face and by its side, and consider which part of the cork has made this shape.

- *Faces of 3D shapes.* Posting boxes are a good example of this concept, with their posting slots which match one face of a 3D shape. Children find, by trial and error to begin with, which shape fits where. As they become familiar with the task, they compare the surface shape, the 2D outline of the 3D shape, with the posting slots, and find a fit. Similarly, printing with 3D shapes (see above) offers similar opportunities of comparing the faces of 3D shapes with their 2D outline.

Reflection and symmetry

Pushing shapes into a posting box, placing shapes into an inset puzzle board, and seeing their reflection in the mirror as themselves are all examples of experiences which children may well have had by the time they are three years old. Young children do not discriminate between left and right, so that mirror images of objects such as shoes have little meaning for them. Until children are five or six years old they are as likely to put their shoes onto the correct feet as the wrong way round. By trial and error they may find how a puzzle piece fits into an inset tray or into a simple jigsaw, turning pieces around and over until there is a fit. When outside, or going for a walk, they can be encouraged to observe symmetry in nature, such as butterflies, or in manufactured items, for example symmetry in railings, wire fencing, or manhole covers. The following examples give an indication of the range of experiences which are appropriate for children of nursery age and which will help them to begin to understand about reflections and symmetry.

- *Turning:* developing ideas of movement, turning and flipping over. Using posting boxes gives early ideas of symmetry, as children find how to turn the shapes in order to fit them through the holes. As they look at the face of the shape they will see a mirror image of the hole through which it has to pass in order to fit. Similarly inset boards can be used. Some of these have been made so that shapes will fit in just one way; for others the shapes will fit in more than one way. Children experience matching the shape by turning it until it fits, and sometimes flipping it over. Jigsaws can be used as a later development. Here the pieces fit together and there are picture as well as shape and symmetry clues.

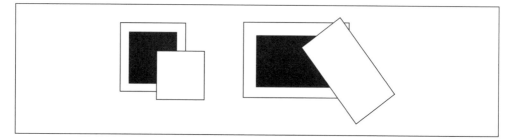

Figure 4.5 The square piece will fit back into its outline in four ways, whereas the rectangle piece will only fit back in two ways

- *Reflections.* Children love to dress up, put on make-up and wear jewellery. When they have finished they often admire their reflection in the mirror. Discussion with an adult can encourage them to make observations about themselves and others that they see in the mirror. They can compare the 'sameness' of the two sides of their bodies. Where there is still water there may also be reflections and children will enjoy seeing their reflection in a puddle or in the water tray.
- *Making symmetrical patterns* (Figures 4.6–4.8). When painting, children can make blot and fold patterns, open out their sheets of paper and discuss the symmetry of the pattern.

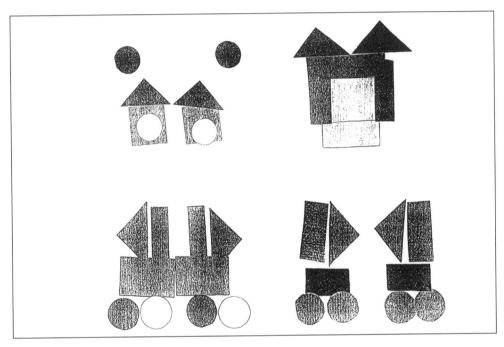

Figure 4.6 Children aged between four years nine months and five years produced these symmetrical pictures from gummed paper shapes

Position and movement

Young children will climb to the top of the climbing frame, hang upside down from a bar, lie on their tummies to view minibeasts, wiggle through a plastic tunnel, crawl around inside crates and boxes, all the time taking note of how the world around them appears to change as they take different positions. They will move in different directions and in different ways, moving backwards, forwards and sideways. They crouch down or stretch up tall, curl up tight or stretch as far as they can. They can be encouraged to develop language of position and movement through such activities. The following shows the range of experiences which will help to develop these concepts:

- *Observing and describing things from different spatial viewpoints.* Encouraging children to observe and describe things they can see from usual and unusual positions, such

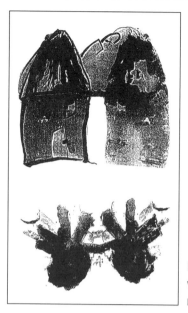

Figure 4.7 These symmetrical blot and fold pictures were produced by Kara, aged four years eleven months, and Michael, four years eleven months

Figure 4.8 Sian, four years ten months, produced this by folding, cutting out and opening up her symmetrical designs

as looking through their legs, from the swing, from the top of the slide, lying on their backs and looking up, will help them to begin to see objects from different spatial points of view. Opportunities will arise spontaneously during children's play and during a focused physical activity, such as a movement session, or through action rhymes. If photographs are taken and displayed of everyday objects from unusual views, for example objects viewed from the outdoor sand pit, the swings, the plastic tunnel, or from the top of the slide, children can look at the photographs and decide where they think they were taken. During a walk there can be opportunities to stop and view familiar things from unfamiliar positions and children can observe what looks the same and how things look different. When children have made a model, perhaps a tower with blocks, they can be encouraged to draw it from the front, then move their position and draw it from another position. Similarly, they may like to draw a favourite toy, the doll's house or a car from different positions. Through discussion with an adult they can compare their drawings for similarities and differences.

- *Relative positions, directions and distances.* Children will be beginning to use position, direction and distance vocabulary such as on, off, on top of, underneath, in front of, near, far away, next to, from, into, out of . . . Sometimes they will have opportunities to choose from a variety of appropriate position language to describe what they see, for example 'My teddy is under the blanket', 'My teddy is in the cot' or 'My teddy is next to the rabbit'. Any of these sentences can describe the situation which they see. With sensitive intervention, an adult can extend the child's awareness of the range of position language that might be used. There will be opportunities to describe movement: 'Jamie is running towards the tree' or 'John is going into the tunnel'. Relative positions can be described so that children become aware of situations where language such as close, next to, and far away, is used. Sometimes the language can be confusing, for example, if 'close to' is used to describe two children sitting together with a 30 cm gap between them or it is used to describe next-door houses, with a much larger distance between them. At this stage children may still be confused if a barrier is placed between themselves and an object and they will then perceive the object as being further away. The concepts of position, direction and distance can be explored through the children's movement and through using the programmable toys PIP or Roamer. They can explore both their own position in relation to things around them and the position of an object in relation to other things (Figures 4.9 and 4.10).

Figure 4.9 A road plan mat enables children to explore movements of straight and turn

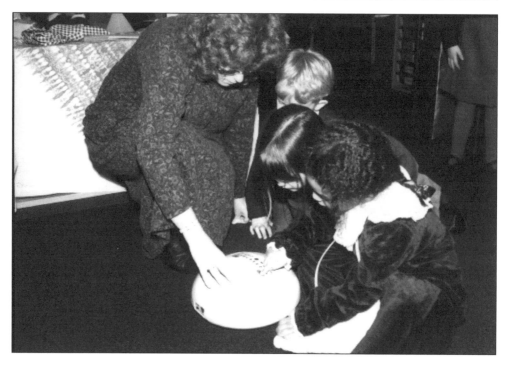

Figure 4.10 Lisa and Neila were shown how to move Roamer forwards

Interpreting pictorial representations of spatial relationships

Through discussing pictures in books and photographs children will begin to understand the relationships between objects in pictures. At this age perspective is not understood and they are just beginning to see how 3D objects are portrayed on paper as 2D objects. Six and seven year old children may still not understand 2D representations of 3D objects. However, when children have opportunities to study pictures and photographs, and make their own paintings and drawings, they can begin to interpret spatial relationships in 2D representations. They can be encouraged to develop their understanding through:

- *Describing pictures of 3D objects.* Children will usually describe what they can see; for example, a man, a dog, or a car. They may describe a bird, but not its position in the tree or the sky. Through discussion with adults their use and understanding of positional language can be enhanced.
- *Modelling things in pictures.* This will help children to make close and detailed observation of what is in the picture and to begin to interpret 2D representations in 3D modelling. They may copy the stance of a person in a picture, or make a model with blocks or construction kit pieces from a picture or photograph. They may wish to use the blocks from a tower and draw around them, using a face to represent each block, as a means of recording (Gura, 1992).
- *Describing their own pictures of objects.* Children will not produce drawings which take account of perspective at this stage. 3D objects will have a 2D view of them;

a person will be drawn from the front view, a box will be an enclosure, a ball will be a circle, and a house will be a front view. Discussion will help children to observe the position from which they have drawn objects and to relate this to distance and direction (Figures 4.11 and 4.12).

Figure 4.11 Drawings of a box, by Hannah and Courtney in Year R, and Victoria and Tom in Year 3. Note how ideas about perspective are beginning to be developed in the drawings by Victoria and Tom, whereas Hannah has drawn a square to represent the box. Courtney shows the interior with a smaller square

Problem-solving

Through their block play, working with construction kits and building models, children will set themselves problems and find ways of solving them. They will make a model, then take it apart to make it in a different way, perhaps changing its shape or its size or both to make it fulfil its purpose. For model making they can be encouraged to develop their problem-solving skills by:

- describing and/or drawing a plan of what they wish to make;
- choosing the materials to make the model, refining their choice as they work;
- carrying out their plan, with adult intervention to discuss how closely their model fits their original planning, and the reasons for changes made;
- reviewing the finished model, describing how they made it, which pieces were chosen and why, and identifying improvements which could be made;

- making and evaluating the improvements to their model;
- using appropriately the language of shape, position and movement in their discussions.

For other aspects of spatial awareness children can be encouraged to describe what they plan to do in order to solve a problem, such as moving from one place to another or finishing a jigsaw puzzle, using appropriate mathematical language.

Block play

Block play has been popular in nursery education for many years. Commercially produced blocks were available during the nineteenth century (Hewitt, 2001). Playing with blocks offers children the opportunity to build their own structures and to explore the properties of both 3D and 2D shapes. Good quality provision for block play includes:

- A generous supply of blocks, easily accessible and well presented
- Clearly defined and well sited block areas with smooth floor surfaces
- Adequate time and space to play
- Freedom of choice to choose where to play
- Unit and hollow blocks the main focus in the area
- A rich display of books and/or pictures to stimulate children's ideas
- Opportunities for risk taking
- Adults who understand and appreciate the value of block play and what is needed to enrich it
- The regular presence of an adult in the block area to support the children in their play

(Cubey, 1999)

Block play can be enhanced by children bringing into the play items from elsewhere; for example, making a bridge and running toy cars across it.

Concept map (Table 4.1)

This shows the concepts outlined above in matrix form. Some example activities are shown so that the map can be used as a basis for planning. Some assessment checkpoints and key questions are given to show possible learning outcomes from the activities (and see Section 4.5).

4.4 Planning shape and space experiences

Adult intervention in children's play

Throughout Section 4.3 above, the importance of sensitive adult intervention in order to introduce and extend children's shape, space and position vocabulary has been stressed. Many of the experiences that children have will come from their own choice, such as working with the blocks, choosing to make a model with a

Table 4.1 Concept map for shape, space and position

Key concept	Vocabulary	Examples of activities	Assessment checkpoints	Key questions
Describe natural and manufactured shapes	Texture: smooth, soft, hard, rough, bumpy, sharp, has points . . .; colour names, features: inside, outside, holes, twists . . .; same, different, similar . . .	Sorting natural from manufactured items: shells, stones, leaves, dolls, cups, books . . .; sorting by colour; sorting by feature: curved from flat faces; shapes with insides from solids; describing similarities and differences	• Sorts consistently for one/two property/ies • Uses vocabulary of texture, colour and feature appropriately • Describes similarities and differences	• Which group does this belong to? Why? How do you know? • What is the same about these? How are they different?
Construct and deconstruct shapes by fitting together, taking apart, rearranging and reshaping	Position: on top, under, beside, next to . . .; it: inside, outside; same, different, similar	Using: stack/nest toys; jigsaws. Making and changing with: blocks; dough; construction kits; shape tiles; cooking; a tent from blankets . . .; describing similarities and differences; making decisions, asking what if . . .? questions	• Fits pieces together and takes them apart • Makes and describes models using appropriate mathematical vocabulary • Plans what to make and how; revises plan to improve model	• Which pieces fit together? Can you make them fit together in a different way? • Can you make a different model with the same pieces? • How can you make your model better?
Simple properties of 3D shapes	Shapes: ball, box, can, tube; cube, pyramid, sphere, cone; face: curved, flat, points, edges, straight . . .; movement: rolling, sliding . . .; arrangements: stacking, building; hollow; insides, outsides, unfolding, folding	Building constructions: finding good shapes for making models; making models: solid, hollow, folding and unfolding paper, blankets; throwing balls, quoits, coming down the slide . . .	• Uses shape vocabulary to describe properties • Uses movement vocabulary to describe properties of shapes	• Which shapes have flat/ curved faces? • What could you make with these shapes? What else could you make? • Which shapes will roll? How could we find out?
Lines, patterns and directions	Straight, curved, zigzag, loop . . .; thick, thin, narrow, wide . . .; shape, turn, straight, bend . . .; forward, backward, straight on, turn	Sand play, printing, painting, drawing, computer art software, sewing: making lines, patterns, thicknesses, directions, outlines . . .; using Roamer or Pip to tell a story: moving in different directions; using the pen adapter to show the pathway	• Discriminates between line shapes and patterns • Uses shape and movement vocabulary to describe line patterns	• What patterns can you make in the sand? What other patterns could you make? What could you use to make them? • How could you make Roamer go over there?
Simple properties of 2D shapes	Circle, triangle, square, rectangle, star; round, straight, flat, point, curved, edge, face, circle, square, triangle . . .	Using shape tiles: making pictures and patterns; describing the shapes; sorting tiles by those with points, curves, straight sides, sorting moons from stars . . . using 3D shapes: comparing their faces; using posting boxes, printing with 3D shapes to compare faces	• Sorts consistently by properties of 2D shapes • Uses shape vocabulary to describe properties	• Describe this shape to a friend: can they guess what it is? • What shape will you see if you print with this?

Table 4.1 (continued)

Reflection and symmetry	Turning: move, turn, flip over	Using shape tiles, jigsaw puzzles: turning, flipping pieces to find a fit . . .; looking in the mirror: describing what can be seen; using the mirror to put on face paints; making symmetrical patterns: printing; blot and fold; cutting folded paper shapes; mirroring movements . . .	• Uses flips and turns to find a fit • Uses vocabulary of reflection and symmetry to describe patterns, pictures and shapes	• What can you see in the mirror? (Blot and fold) What do you think you will see when you open up your paper? • Can you copy your partner's movements?
Position and movement	On, off, on top of, underneath, in front of, near, far away, next to, from, into, out of . . .	Using climbing apparatus/ movement sessions: describing movements, positions from the top/bottom/part way up the slide; looking between legs; lying on tummy; using Roamer or Pip: moving in different directions; predicting where Roamer will go . . .; describing relative position of toys: in the doll's house, cars on the road plan . . .	• Uses vocabulary of position and movement • Follows instructions which use position and movement vocabulary • Makes observations from different viewpoints	• What can you see? What do you think you will see if you look between your legs? • Where will you go if you move forward/sideways . . .? • How can we make Roamer go to the cupboard?
Interpret pictorial representations of spatial relationships	Describing pictures of 3D objects; describing their own pictures of objects	Looking at pictures in books/ pictures they have drawn: describing objects using shape and position vocabulary; making a model from a picture	• Uses vocabulary of shape and position to describe objects in a picture • Observes/draws objects from different positions and identifies similarities and differences	• What can you see in the picture? Where is it? What is next to the . . .? • What if you draw it from over there? How will it look the same/ different?
Use developing mathematical ideas and methods to solve practical problems	Pattern, puzzle; What could we try next? How did you work it out?	Making models, pictures or patterns using 2D and/or 3D shapes; moving Roamer from one place to another	• Makes models or drawings and describes them using appropriate vocabulary • Moves from one place to another and describes what has been done	• What other models/pictures could you make? • What other materials could you use? • How could you make this even better? • How did you work it out? • What could we try next?

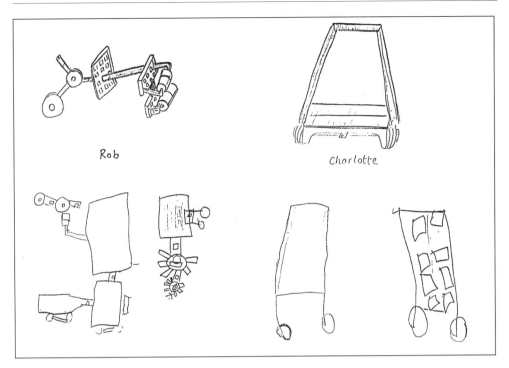

Figure 4.12 Children, aged four years ten months, made models from a construction kit then drew their models from two different views. These drawings are shown alongside sketches made of the same models by student teachers

construction kit, deciding they want to make plasticine cakes. All of these experiences offer opportunities for children's awareness of spatial concepts and language to be enhanced. It is important that adults' own understanding of the concepts outlined above is secure, so that children listen to the appropriate language from the adult. Sometimes children hear 3D shapes named by a face, such as a brick as a 'square' or a cylinder as a 'circle', which is confusing for the child and should be avoided.

Focused activities

Planned activities for developing spatial concepts will frequently include opportunities to develop several concepts, rather than just concentrating upon one aspect. The following activities demonstrate both planning for a range of concepts, and activities which concentrate upon just one concept.

Making jigsaws

An activity for a group of four children:

- *Purpose:* to develop understanding of 2D shape, symmetry and movement.
- *Materials:* pictures from celebration cards, such as Christmas, birthday or Eid, safety scissors, envelopes to store each home-made jigsaw.
- *Language:* shape, turn, turn over, move, fit . . .

How to begin

Each child chooses a card and makes one cut across the card to make two pieces. The cuts can be straight, curved or jagged. They move the two pieces apart and fit them back together again, then swap their jigsaws with each other. Discussion can include:

- What shapes have you made?
- Who has a curved/straight/jagged edge?
- Where does this piece fit?
- What happens if we turn this over? Does it fit now?

This activity can be repeated, this time making two or three cuts in the cards to make three or four pieces.

Clearing up

An activity for a group or for everyone as part of circle time. This can be repeated over time, with one or two new words introduced each time:

- *Purpose:* to develop understanding of the language of position and movement.
- *Materials:* items to be put away.
- *Language:* straight, turn, near, far, underneath, on top, over, behind, in front, up, down . . .

How to begin

The adult chooses an item and a child to put it away. The child follows the adult's instructions, whilst the others watch. All the children will need to face into the classroom so that they all observe in the same direction as the adult. Putting away a bucket under the sand tray could include:

Go behind the doll's house.
Now go round the paint table.
Turn to the sand tray. Now walk to it.
The bucket goes underneath. That's right. On the shelf under the tray.

Or, for putting a puzzle on a display table:

Go to the blocks; they're behind the books.
Now, turn to the window. Go to the table.
Put the puzzle in front of the dominoes.

As the children become more confident, they can take turns to give each other instructions for putting things away.

I-spy

An activity for a small group or the whole class during circle time:

- *Purpose:* to develop understanding of simple properties of shapes.
- *Materials:* items on a tray which can be seen by the children, such as a ball, box, spring, shell, bracelet . . .
- *Language:* round, straight, curved, corner, edge, flat . . .

How to begin

The adult describes an item on the tray and the children decide which one it is:

- I spy something which is round and smooth. It doesn't have any corners. What is it?
- I spy something which has flat faces. You can put things inside it. What is it?
- I spy something curved, smooth, with a hole in it. What is it?

Children can take turns to describe items on the tray for the others to recognise.

Alternatively, with a small group of children, a feely bag or box can be used, and either children find items to fit a description, or they describe what they can feel.

Block play

An activity for four children:

- *Purpose:* to design and build a structure.
- *Materials:* large wooden blocks, picture books, paper and pencils or crayons.
- *Language:* flat, curved, edge . . .

How to begin

Children discuss with an adult what they will make. They give as detailed a description as possible, perhaps showing a picture in a book of what they would like to do. Sometimes children can draw a picture of their intentions. The adult asks questions to encourage the planning process:

- Which blocks will be best to make the wall?
- Why will you choose those?
- What will you put on top?

When the model is made, ask the children questions to compare the finished model with what was planned:

- You've used these blocks instead. Why did you choose these?
- I like the curved shapes on top of the wall. Did you try any other shapes?

Encourage the children to draw their finished model, helping them to observe which blocks they have used, so that their drawing is as accurate as possible. If time permits, they can draw their model from different views.

Making models

An activity for four to six children:

- *Purpose:* to explore making and reshaping 3D models.
- *Materials:* playdough or plasticine, boards, clay tools.
- *Language:* outside, inside, side, flat, curved, straight . . .

How to begin

Ask the children what they would like to make, perhaps using that week's theme as the starting point. As they work discuss their models using shape language:

- What a wiggly snake! He curves around the board.
- What will you put inside the vase?
- Do you want to make a pattern on the outside of your vase?

When the models are finished, encourage the children to describe their own and each other's models. Remind them of their original intentions; ask about changes they have made. Discuss possible improvements and as they make changes ask them to describe what they are doing:

- I'm making round apples for my tree.
- The dog needs a long, wiggly lead.
- Straight flowers for the vase.

Printing

An activity for four children:

- *Purpose:* to explore lines.
- *Materials:* items for printing, such as feathers, sponges, strips of stiff card, toothbrushes, printing pad and paints, paint brushes, paper.
- *Language:* straight, curved, loop, wavy, zigag, thick, thin . . .

How to begin

Ask the children to make prints on the paper, choosing different items. Compare the shapes and lines that they make:

- What did you use to make the thin straight lines?
- How can we make zigzags?
- What sort of shapes will the toothbrush make?

As the children begin to recognise how they can make various types of lines and shapes, they can design their own line patterns.

Involving adult helpers in the planned activities

Language associated with spatial concepts is also language used in everyday life. This language should be used correctly and in appropriate contexts. The language to be developed can be included on the weekly planning sheet and during planning sessions. Some adults may well, in their everyday conversations, misuse spatial language. It is important to encourage its correct usage, such as not confusing 3D shapes with their faces (calling a box a square for example). Where adults are involved with helping children to record their models by drawing or through making a data handling chart, it is important to remember that at this stage children will not be able to draw 3D representations of shapes; rather they will draw 2D representations, such as an enclosure for a square, circle or rectangle and for a cube, sphere, and so on. Other recording methods can be used, such as placing real objects onto recording sheets, rather than risk confusing children perhaps by recording a picture of a circle when the object was a ball. In order to ensure that all adults working in the nursery during that week are aware of any specific requirements with regard to language and recording, it is helpful to spend a few minutes before the start of each session agreeing the strategies to be adopted.

Shape and space activities for nursery environments (Table 4.2)

Table 4.2 Shape and space activities for nursery environments

Environment	Concept/skill	Context
circle time	• explore line shapes and patterns	• playing traditional nursery games, e.g. Farmer's in his den, Looby Loo . . .
art and craft particular areas	• sort by shape • explore symmetry • fit together, take apart • explore line shapes and patterns • explore properties of 2D shapes • interpret pictorial representations of spatial relationships	• choosing printing block to produce shape • choosing item to print particular line • making symmetrical blot and fold pattern • making and reshaping dough models • taking apart/remaking cardboard boxes • folding sheets of paper • making line patterns by drawing, printing, painting . . . • making pictures and patterns by painting, drawing, printing . . . • making pictures of real objects
table top games and collections	• fit together, take apart • explore properties of 2D shapes • explore symmetry	• making jigsaws • making pictures and patterns with shape tiles • threading and changing beads, making and changing 'poppet' necklaces • using shape posting boxes
sand play	• sort by shape • explore line shapes and patterns • explore properties of 2D shapes	• sorting sand play items by shape • making line patterns in the sand • making shape outline patterns in the sand
construction	• sort by shape: same and different • sort by properties of shape • fit together, take apart • interpret pictorial representations of spatial relationships	• choosing construction pieces by shape • choosing construction pieces by property of shape, e.g. 'curved'. • exploring which pieces make 'strong' structures • making a model, taking it apart and re-making in a different shape • making a drawn plan for a model • using a drawing/picture to make a model • drawing a picture of a model

Table 4.2 (continued)

block play	<ul><li>sort by shape: same and different</li><li>sort by properties of shape</li><li>fit together, take apart</li><li>explore properties of shapes</li><li>explore line shapes and patterns</li><li>interpret pictorial representations of spatial relationships</li></ul>	<ul><li>choosing blocks by shape</li><li>choosing construction pieces by property of shape, e.g. 'curved'.</li><li>exploring which pieces make 'strong' structures</li><li>making a model, taking it apart and remaking in a different shape</li><li>running items down a ramp</li><li>making lines of blocks: straight, turn . . .</li><li>making a drawn plan for a model</li><li>using a drawing/picture to make a model</li><li>drawing a picture of a model</li></ul>
role play	<ul><li>sort by colour, texture,</li><li>explore reflection</li><li>explore properties of shapes</li><li>explore position and movement</li></ul>	<ul><li>choosing dressing-up clothes</li><li>choosing jewellery by shape of beads</li><li>observing reflection in a mirror</li><li>using a mirror to put on facepaints</li><li>folding blankets, sheets, tablecloths</li><li>moving furniture and goods to rearrange the shop/café/kitchen . . .</li></ul>
miniworlds	<ul><li>explore position and movement</li></ul>	<ul><li>moving dolls and furniture in the doll's house/boats on the marina/cars on the road plan . . .</li></ul>
outside play	<ul><li>explore properties of shapes</li><li>explore line shapes and patterns</li><li>explore position and movement</li></ul>	<ul><li>throwing and rolling balls, hoops, quoits . . .</li><li>playing traditional movement games, e.g. Hokey Cokey . . .</li><li>climbing/swinging from apparatus</li><li>moving on trucks and tricycles</li><li>moving toys using trucks</li></ul>
cooking	<ul><li>explore spatial properties</li></ul>	<ul><li>making cakes and biscuits in different shapes</li><li>cutting out pastry and biscuit dough using various shaped cutters</li><li>decorating cakes with different shaped items</li></ul>
information technology	<ul><li>explore 2D shapes and their properties</li><li>explore line shapes and patterns</li><li>interpret pictorial representations of spatial relationships</li></ul>	<ul><li>using an art software package to draw lines, shapes</li><li>making Roamer/Pip travel in a straight line/turn</li><li>using pen adapter with Roamer and observing Roamer's path</li></ul>

4.5 Assessment

Use the assessment checkpoints and key questions in Table 4.1 to help with assessment. The questions include both closed (how many?) and open (how do you know?) types. Observations, with evidence of the child's behaviour to support their understanding, can be recorded. Where evidence of achievement in a standard form is required, the observational evidence can be supported by a note of the assessment checkpoint, with date and comment attached to show when the evidence of achievement was noted. Regular observation of children's use of spatial concepts will identify their current knowledge and skills. This may identify whether children can:

- describe natural and manufactured shapes, using appropriate mathematical and everyday language;
- construct and deconstruct shapes, describing what has been made and the shapes used and formed;
- identify and use simple properties of 3D shapes to sort, classify and identify suitable shapes to solve problems;
- make and name types of lines, such as straight or curved;
- identify and name simple properties of 2D shapes;
- recognise reflections and symmetry in patterns and pictures, using appropriate language;
- experience, observe and describe using the language of position and movement.

Opportunities to make such assessments may occur incidentally during children's chosen activity or through specifically targeted focused activity.

Children respond well to questions such as:

- What is the same about these? How are they different?
- Who has more/fewer?

especially where they have been encouraged to respond using the mathematical vocabulary that they hear the adults using. Gradually they begin to respond in sentences and this should be encouraged.

What three and four year olds find more difficult are questions which ask 'How do you know?' such as:

- Which group does this belong to? Why? How do you know?

Here the children tend not to respond to the third question. PGCE students trialled some of the key questions in 2001 and discovered that young children did not cope well with this sort of question. However, with practice, and with examples of how they might answer given by adults, they do begin to answer the 'How do you know?' type of question in a satisfactory way.

Possible errors in concepts of shape and space

Children's understanding of spatial concepts will be limited by their awareness of topological concepts. These include:

- Enclosures used to represent any closed shape, such as circle, square, triangle. Children may only just begin to recognise the differences between a circle and a triangle whilst in the nursery. This will be reflected in their drawings of shapes.
- Judgements of proximity and separation are influenced by barriers. A child may say that the blocks are near the window until a chair is placed between the window and the blocks. Then they will believe that the blocks and the window

are further apart, even though these have not moved.

- Fitting things together, such as completing a puzzle, may still be by trial and error, rather than observing the shape and how to turn it to make a fit.
- A line with bricks or buttons may not be straight unless there is a straight edge to act as a guide, for example the table edge. Children may not perceive that their line is crooked, and may have difficulty distinguishing 'straight' in 2D and 3D shapes.
- Misunderstanding of language of distance, unless the context is clear: 'near' relating to two children sitting next to each other, and 'near' as in relation to grandma living nearby, perhaps in the next street.

The above errors are, in Piagetian terms, to do with developmental processes and children will understand these concepts in time. Further experiences of the concepts and opportunities to explore materials will enable children to begin to build their schemas for these concepts to enhance their understanding.

4.6 Working in partnership with parents and carers

Parents will be involved in helping their children to develop spatial concepts throughout the early years. Children will hear language of shape, position and movement being used, and will begin to use it themselves, both through activities in the nursery and through the home.

Activities at home for developing understanding of spatial concepts

These activities do not require any special equipment as they make use of everyday items in the home.

Sorting shapes
- *Putting away the shopping:* sorting out the tins, the boxes.
- *I-spy games:* finding shapes the same such as cylinders, balls or spheres.
- *Putting toys away:* sorting the Lego bricks into sets of 'same shape'; sorting the toy cars from the lorries.
- *On visits:* finding and sorting shells at the seaside; pebbles; leaves; sorting conkers, acorns and sycamore 'helicopters'.

Exploring shapes
- *Using construction kits:* Lego and Sticklebrick models; plasticine models; describing the shapes.
- *Cooking:* making pastry shapes; using pastry cutters.
- *Cutting out:* cutting around pictures, following the outline; cutting up pictures to make a jigsaw puzzle.
- *Puzzles:* using posting toys, inset puzzles, simple jigsaws.

Drawing

- *At home:* drawing favourite toys, family members, the trees in the garden, the view from the window.
- *Lines:* drawing line patterns: straight, curved, wiggly, zigzag.

Reflections

- *Mirrors:* describing what can be seen in looking glasses, car mirrors and the bowls of spoons.
- *Outside:* looking in puddles and ponds and describing reflections.

Going for walks

- *Position:* looking at things and describing where they are: the house on top of the hill; the chimneys on the roof; the tunnel under the road; the things in the shop.
- *Movement:* using language to explain where we are going, for example, out of the door, across the street, turn the corner and down the hill.

CHAPTER 5
Measure – Making Comparisons

The *Curriculum Guidance for the Foundation Stage* (DfEE, 2000) identifies the following key objectives for children to reach by the end of the reception stage:

- Use language such as 'greater', 'smaller', 'heavier' or 'lighter' to compare quantities.
- Use developing mathematical ideas and methods to solve practical problems.

To be able to measure is a life skill, and one that will be used in various contexts throughout life. For a child, comparisons of size are important, such as who has the longer pencil, larger teddy or taller sandcastle. A teenager will be concerned with clothes and sizes, finding a good fit, understanding the sizing system and how that applies to them, and being able to measure with reasonable accuracy, and making estimates of size. For an adult, good measuring skills are important in industry, where very fine degrees of accuracy are used. Adults use their estimation skills when making purchases for the home, and will measure for household items such as curtains, carpets or shelving, in order to make successful purchases. In Britain the complexities of measuring are compounded by our use of a dual system of measuring units; although industry now uses metric units, many adults still use imperial measures for home use.

Measuring can never be exact. This is a fundamental principle of measures, which is not always understood by adults. A measure is always an approximation, and the degree of accuracy used, such as to the nearest one, tenth, hundredth or thousandth of a centimetre, reflects the notion of approximation. To be effective at measuring, children will need to acquire skills of estimation, choosing units, using measuring instruments, and making measures to an appropriate degree of accuracy for the task. Measuring involves using numbers and number operations in real situations.

It has been argued (Ainley, 1991, for example; though she changes her view later in the article) that there is 'very little mathematical thinking' involved in measuring. The view that is adopted in this chapter is that measuring does demand thinking skills and is often used in solving problems:

- posing a problem such as 'is the tower tall enough?';
- deciding how to solve the problem, perhaps making an estimate of height, or choosing the units for making a direct measure; deciding upon the degree of accuracy to be used;
- making decisions based upon the data collected from measuring.

Measuring is complex, in that it involves a range of different concepts and the associated skills:

- length
- mass
- capacity
- area
- volume
- time
- compound measures, such as density, and litres per kilometre and miles per hour.

To be able to make informed and effective decisions in adult life, children will learn about each of these aspects of measures, their units of measure and the use of the appropriate measuring tool. Whilst there are links between some of the measures, such as length and area and volume, the skills of measuring for each will need to be learnt.

By the time children start at nursery, they are already using notions of measuring in everyday life. They will be asked questions such as 'How old are you?' 'Have you older brothers and sisters?' Three and four year olds will use measuring language for themselves, such as:

- I'm big! (Meaning, I'm tall.)
- I'm strong. I can lift it by myself.
- Put some more in. I'm thirsty.

Some children will have their growth marked regularly on a height chart at home, and some may help to weigh out ingredients in the kitchen. Nursery experiences will build upon these.

5.1 How children learn about measuring: research findings

Piaget *et al.* (1960) studied children's acquisition of concepts of measurement. He considered in particular how children develop understanding of the measurement of metrical properties of space, in particular length, area and volume. In this book, 'weight', rather than 'mass' is the term used, as it is the one that the children are more likely to hear used in everyday life. The development of understanding of concepts of time is considered separately from the other measures, as the concepts are abstract, rather than based upon objects and circumstances which can be seen. The following discussion is a summary from Piaget *et al.* (1960), Wheeler (1960) and Hohmann *et al.* (1978).

Length and distance, area, volume, capacity, weight

From two to about four years of age

Children make perceptual comparisons of length, through moving their line of vision from one item to another, to see if they are the same. For concepts of distance, Piaget *et al.* found that concepts of proximities are not understood, and that children believe that distances are changed when something is placed between two objects. Children also believe that a journey which is travelled regularly is a short one, probably because it is familiar, whereas an unfamiliar journey is perceived as being longer. With area, by the time they are about four years old, they will compare two equal areas and agree that they are the same size. However, the experiment of Piaget *et al.* with two card fields of equal area and houses placed on them, showed that there was an intuitive response to questions about area, and that children did not perceive two areas as still the same where the same number of toy houses had been placed on both fields, but in different arrangements. Piaget *et al.* found that when dividing up volumes, such as cakes for dolls, children of this age did not make equal shares. A cake might be divided up so that dolls received a piece, but either the pieces were of different sizes, or the dolls were given small quantities and a large piece was left. By about three, children can fit one ordered set of objects to another, such as putting lids on jars. Young children do not understand the difference between volume and capacity. They will pour from one container to another, exploring how much sand or water will fit inside a container.

At about four to five years of age

Children begin to make comparisons of length by making direct comparisons. When two identical sticks are placed in line children will agree that they are the same length. However, when one stick is pushed forward, so that they are now out of alignment, children will usually consider the one pushed forward as being longer. They do not make paired relationships between both ends of the sticks at this stage, merely observing one end, and so do not notice that the ends are not level. They make judgements of relative position rather than comparison of length (Figure 5.1). If asked to put in order of length a set of pencils, children may align one end of each pencil with the others, but may not put them in order from shortest to longest. However, with help, most can do this. Piaget's findings were that most children achieved this by the time they were seven years of age. Children can make comparisons using language such as heavier, lighter, longer, shorter, full, empty, and use superlative language of heaviest, lightest, and so on.

Conservation of these measures is usually understood during primary education:

- Length at between six and a half and seven years.
- Area at about seven to seven and a half.
- Volume at about eight and a half to nine.
- Weight at about nine or ten.

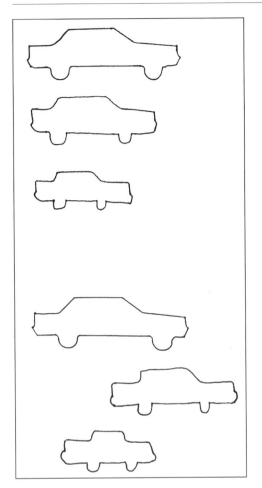

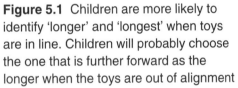

Figure 5.1 Children are more likely to identify 'longer' and 'longest' when toys are in line. Children will probably choose the one that is further forward as the longer when the toys are out of alignment

Time

There are two main, abstract, concepts associated with time:

- the measurement of time on a watch or clock, that is 'the time' that something occurs, such as 4.30 or half past four;
- the passing of time, measured in seconds, minutes, hours, days, weeks, months, seasons, years. Age is an example of this which young children readily accept, for example, that they are a year older with each birthday.

Most children do not conserve time until they are about seven or eight years old (Althouse, 1994). As young children of nursery age they believe that they control the passing of time by the speed of their movements, so that if they run quickly time passes quickly, but if they move slowly so does the passing of time. Until they can separate time from their own movements, children cannot make sense of standard units of time. Concepts of the passing of time have been further analysed into three categories (Charlesworth and Lind, 1990):

- *Personal time.* This refers to past, present and future. Young children find understanding of past and future more difficult than the present, as the former are not part of the child's immediate experience.
- *Social time.* This refers to the sequence of events which makes up the child's daily experience, for example, getting up in the morning, having breakfast, and so on.
- *Cultural time.* This is time measured by clocks and calendars.

5.2 Measuring and key concepts

It will be seen from the above that the major concept of conservation of measures is not acquired during the pre-school years. However, building upon their experiences from home, children can begin to understand concepts of comparison and order related to size; they experience time passing and begin to understand how this can be measured, and to sequence events. Two separate groupings of concepts are considered: those for measures of spatial objects, that is length, weight, capacity, area and volume; and for time.

Key concepts for measures of objects:

- using descriptive language;
- using comparative language;
- making ordered arrangements.

The first two key concepts and the experiences that can help to develop understanding will be considered for length, weight, capacity, area and volume; the third one for length, weight and capacity. Further development of concepts of area and volume are usually left until children are older.

Key concepts for time:

- sequencing events;
- experiencing different rates of speed;
- comparing different units of time.

Using descriptive language

Language such as big, little, small, long, thin and wide can be used to make gross descriptions but it is not specific enough for making comparisons. However, for the very young child, or one whose vocabulary is not well developed, this language needs to become part of everyday speech. All such language is subjective, in that it depends upon the child's experiences which words they might choose to use. A parcel which is heavy to one child may seem light to another; similarly the tall tower may be short compared with what was built the day before.

- *Length.* Children will enjoy sorting objects and then use language of length to describe what they have found, such as big, little, long, short, thin, wide and tall. Opportunities to use such language will arise in all nursery environments, such as when they are using blocks, model making, or painting (Figure 5.2). They can

Figure 5.2 These paintings of themselves were used by the reception class to compare and order heights. The children enjoyed seeing how much they had grown when the paintings were taken down

be encouraged to follow instructions which use the language of length, such as making a block roadway long enough to reach the garage, or cutting long strips of wool to make hair for the puppet. It should be noted that where children make drawings their representations of objects may well not be accurate in terms of height or width. Other considerations seem to come into play here, as demonstrated by Cox and Wright (2000), who looked at five and seven year olds' representations of men and women. It seemed that the children perceived women as taller when they wear a skirt. However, it is important to discuss drawings with children and, where appropriate, to make direct comparisons between their drawings and the objects themselves in order to compare for length. In this way children will begin to make more accurate observations, even if they cannot yet show that in what they draw.

- *Weight*. Weigh, heavy and light will be the language that children will use. They will pick up items and say whether these are heavy or light. They may use scales or a balance to 'weigh' what they have collected, mimicking adult behaviour.
- *Capacity*. Filling containers, pouring water or sand through sieves, funnels or wheels, children will use the words 'full' and 'empty'. Discussion with them as to what is meant by 'full' is helpful, as the mathematical meaning is different from the social one. A cup of tea is full to the point where it can still be safely lifted, whereas when playing in the sand or water, full may mean to the

brim. This can be discussed during snack time, when children pour out their own drink.

- *Area.* Putting a cloth on the table and covering the table with newspaper before painting are two examples where children can be encouraged to use early language of area, such as cover and fits.
- *Volume.* Language such as big, little, large, small and tiny may be used at first to describe the size of containers and boxes, or of models which the children have made. They might sort out the tiny buttons to fit in an egg cup, or put the large pebbles into a pile in the garden.

Using comparative language

In order to give more meaning to the language of size, children should be encouraged to make comparisons of two objects and to consider which is longer, heavier, more full, and so on. The opposite of each of these needs to be used, too, so that children can begin to make comparisons between two items, using longer and shorter, heavier and lighter, and so on. This language, being used during practical situations, will become familiar and understood as its meaning becomes apparent. Children can use the language when estimating, and then make a direct comparison to check.

- *Length.* There is a wide range of comparative vocabulary which can be developed including longer, taller, shorter, wider, narrower, thicker, thinner, about the same . . . Children can be encouraged to make these comparisons, during their play, such as when dressing up and finding a longer or shorter scarf, or when using woodworking tools and looking for a wider piece of wood. Children may choose a plank that is long enough to make a bridge. Older children may place blocks in a line to match the length of a longer one. They can be encouraged to say which is longer/shorter, and how many shorter ones they need to match the length of the longer one.
- *Weight.* Children can use their hands to make estimations of comparisons of weight, lifting an item then another, or holding one in each hand. They can decide which is heavier, and, by implication, which is lighter. They can use a simple balance, putting some bricks into one pan and perhaps some small toys into the other, and observe which is heavier or when they have about the same weight in each pan. Using a balance and pouring into one then the other pan allows the children to experiment with weighing and to observe how the balance operates and that as more is poured into the lighter side it will become heavier than the other. Putting a balance by the sand and water trays will encourage children to use these materials so that they begin to develop the concept of weight associated with free-flowing materials (Figure 5.3). When baking, children can use a 100 g weight and add flour until it balances the weight. They may also use a dial scale, and pour flour until the pointer reaches 100 g.

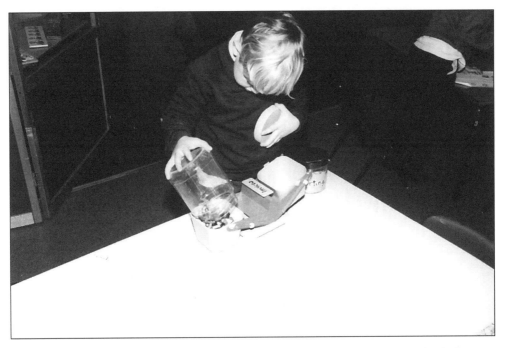

Figure 5.3 Josh poured out all the buttons to see what would happen to the balance

- *Capacity.* When working in the sand or water, pouring drinks in the home area or café, or at snack time, children can make comparisons of how much is in a container. Language such as more, less, about the same, empty, full, nearly full, nearly empty, can be developed. Children can compare two containers and say 'This is nearly full; this one has less.' The comparisons will not necessarily be opposites, as the language of full and empty without some qualification is unlikely to be appropriate. They can pour from a jug into two cups to make both have the same, and pour out from a jug until they have found how many cups it will fill. The difference between filling a cup for drinking, and filling a cup to the brim should be discussed. Children will probably observe that they spill water from cups filled to the brim (Figure 5.4).
- *Area.* Children's understanding of area develops later than that of length. Language which can be developed at this early stage includes more than, less than, cover, fit, too much, not enough . . . Children can be encouraged to place a book on another to see if they take up the same amount of space, or to choose a sheet of paper to cover another. They can discuss which one is larger or smaller. When making junk models, they can discuss which box needs more paint to cover it (surface area).
- *Volume.* The language of size, fit, too big, too small . . . can be developed through making comparisons. Comparing two models to see which one is larger or smaller will help children to begin to develop the concept of volume. They can use some bricks to build a model, then use the same number of identical bricks to build a different model. Children do not conserve volume until they are

Figure 5.4 These nursery children spent some time pouring from one container into another. They observed the flow of sand carefully

much older; making models from playdough, then using the same piece of playdough to make another model, will begin the process of understanding of conservation of volume. Simple displacement activities will help children to begin to understand what happens to water when an object is dropped into it. They can use language of same, more, different . . . when comparing volumes. Children can match lids to boxes and jars, making comparisons of size to find which fit. In sand play, a colander can be used to separate grains of sand from buttons or small gravel.

Making ordered arrangements

- *Length.* Ask which is the longest, shortest, tallest, widest . . . and encourage children to compare by placing the objects with one end of each in line, so that they can make direct comparisons. When they make such comparisons themselves, it is important to check that they are lining the objects up, as they will look to see which one is furthest in front. They can cut lengths of paper when making models, to match the longest, shortest and widest. Children can be encouraged to find lengths by counting units, for example, putting out a line of bricks which matches the length of a model (Figure 5.5). They can also compare length and width for the size of an object (Figure 5.6).

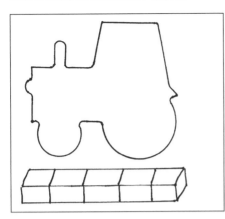

Figure 5.5 Children can match the length of a toy with a line of bricks

Figure 5.6 The children chose the item that they wanted by size

- *Weight.* Children can fill tins or boxes and make their own heaviest or lightest parcel. When working in the shop, they can compare parcels with their hands to estimate which is the heaviest. If large lighter and small heavier parcels are included in the variety available, children can experience that the weight of a parcel cannot be estimated just by looking at it, and that it needs to be picked up and compared with another.
- *Capacity.* When filling containers children can fill one to the top, fill another half full and a third with hardly anything in it. They can describe how full they are, using language such as most, least, nearly empty, nearly full to the top, half full, empty . . . When putting buttons or beads into tins they can be encouraged to

use similar language, so making comparisons, and putting into order how full the containers are.

Time

Sequencing events

The concept of the sequence of events is difficult for young children to grasp, as for them it is the immediacy of 'now' that is important. This concept is about time passing, whether now, the past or predicting the future. Recalling events in order, using past experiences to predict future ones, can be very difficult. Teachers of young children will recognise Mark, aged four years six months, and his request:

Mark: Miss, Miss. Can I put my coat on? It's time to go home.
Teacher: Not yet, Mark. It's time for milk. Then you can put your coat on to go out to play.
Mark: Isn't Mummy coming?
Teacher: At home time. She'll be here later on. Now, it's time for milk.

During milk time, Mark's teacher discussed with all the children the format of the school day, encouraging them to remember what had happened so far that morning and to predict what was to come.

- *Sequencing regular events.* Sequencing regular events will help children such as Mark to recognise features of the day in order to remember what has just happened and predict what is likely to happen next. Children may remember events, but not the order in which they occur. Language such as today, yesterday, morning, afternoon, next, before, after, then, now . . . should be used so that this language becomes familiar in context to the children.
- *Describing past events.* What happened yesterday? When was your birthday? How old were you? What did you do at the weekend? These are examples of social questions that are asked. Young children often will not remember, or not recall the sequence of events, or not have a relevant vocabulary, so that going on holiday was 'yesterday' rather than some months previously. Children can be encouraged to recall past events, describing what they have done or seen. When special events occur in the nursery it can help children to remember this at a later date if photographs are taken, then placed in sequence in a book. A photographic record of individual children and their activities over time can be very useful as it will lead to discussions of changes in height and appearance, clothing changes with the seasons, recalling past events and what occurred. Language of the past, including days of the week, ages, special events and festivals, before, then, next, after . . . can be developed to help children to be more precise in their recall (Figure 5.7).
- *Predicting future events.* Language such as tomorrow, next week, the days of the week, at the weekend . . ., where children describe what they hope will happen, encourages understanding of what is meant by the future. Children can be

Figure 5.7 Each child drew a picture and stuck it to their birthday carriage. This means of handling and recording data acted as a reminder for birthdays

encouraged to plan what they intend to do next in the nursery, both orally and by drawing a picture, then to recall what they have done and compare it with their prediction. Similarly, they can predict what they will do at home, then compare their prediction with their recall of events the next day. When being read a favourite story, children can predict what will happen next, then hear the next part of the story and compare their version with that from the book. They can help to plan special events, or celebration of festivals, through discussion, photographs of past events, and making drawings of what they would like to happen. A count-down chart to a special event, such as an Advent calendar, will help to mark how many days have passed and how many are to come before the event. If a child is to have a birthday during the week, then they may like to bake a cake ready for their birthday for the others to share.

Experiencing different rates of speed

Young children do not understand the relationship between time and rate (Hohmann *et al.*, 1978). If building a tower of blocks was harder work than building a roadway, or if the tower used more blocks than the roadway, then they believe that building the tower took longer. If two children run to the climbing frame, one having a head start, but both arriving together, another child will insist that they ran at the same speed. They cannot isolate the two movements to make comparisons of speed. However, they can use notions of speed, moving slowly and quickly, during a movement session, and this can be used to help them to begin to understand the relationship between speed and time.

- *Experiencing different rates of speed.* Children will enjoy using wheeled toys; toys that roll or spin; equipment that moves such as ropes, swings, seesaws; and things that can drip or pour, such as paint, glue, sand and water. They can use these items and observe how they move, and try to change their speed, and describe what they observe, using language such as start, stop, slow, slowly, slowest, fast, faster, fastest, quick, quickly, quickest. During movement sessions they can be encouraged to move more quickly, or more slowly, and in music sessions play instruments to keep time, play them more quickly or more slowly. They will begin to understand that rates of speed can be changed, and that when events occur at different speeds their finishing times will be different.

Comparing different units of time

Telling the time is a skill which most children acquire at about eight years of age. During the last twenty years, with the advent of digital time in household appliances such as video recorders, hi-fi systems and cookers, many young children will be aware that such timers are important in their families' lives, and that they are used to ensure that certain events happen, such as recording a favourite television programme, or ensuring that food is reheated properly in the microwave oven. Young children may be aware that the time is 'told' on clocks by numbers, but they are unlikely to have any sense of what this means.

A six year old at school, who had just had his birthday, showed his teacher his new watch:

Jamie: Look. It says 10.59.
Teacher: What will it say in one minute?
Jamie: 10.60.

Jamie had learnt to read the numerals, and knew that 60 followed 59 but this did not mean that he understood how to tell the time.

For young children, there will be both digital and analogue clocks at home, and these will have no real meaning for them yet. However, certain times of the day may be very important to them, in that the time represents something special, such as a favourite television programme, or the time that they will be collected from nursery.

- *Recognising special clock and calendar times.* Calling attention to the nursery clock, at snack time, at home time, will give children experience of clocks as a measure of the time. The numbers on the clock may be read, and the position of the hands noted for important times. Children can begin to recognise certain times, such as 'twelve o'clock and it's time to go home'. A calendar in the nursery, marking the days of the week, and perhaps the date, will help children to recognise the regular sequence of the days. Birthday charts, with the months marked, will introduce the months in order. A count-down calendar, to mark the timing of a future special event, will help to show the passage of time. This work is just the beginning of recognising that clocks and calendars are used by society to mark the passing of time and that such instruments can be read. They will not yet understand these standard units of time, as they are too abstract. However, such language is part of everyday conversation and children can begin to use some of it with understanding, such as 'today is Tuesday and tomorrow will be Wednesday'. Language to be introduced can include days of the week, the months, o'clock times, minutes, hours, days . . .

- *Comparing units of time.* Children can use clocks, watches, sand timers, rocker timers and water timers as part of everyday life. Watching the sand pour through the sand timer, then turning it over and watching it again, then using the timer to mark a well-defined period of time, such as putting some toys away, will help them to begin to appreciate the duration of that period of time. A clock in the home area may be set by the children to show breakfast time, or lunch time, and be included in their play. 'In about an hour' or 'in two weeks' time' have no meaning as units of time are not understood by young children. Relating periods of time to real events helps children to begin to appreciate time intervals, such as 'by the time you have put the toys away it will be milk time' or 'when the daffodil bulbs have grown their flowers it will be your birthday'. A regular, recurring sequence of events in the nursery day will help children to make sense of the passage of time when they are away from home.

Problem-solving

Children can use their growing understanding of measures through planning, carrying out and evaluating the results. If they choose to make a roadway for some cars, they will make decisions about how long it should be, how wide, whether there is room for two cars to pass each other . . . In making the roadway, they will choose which blocks to use, deciding upon their size: length, width and depth. When using Roamer or Pip they will make estimates of how far to send the programmable toy in order to reach its destination, and may use addition to help them: 'We put in 3, but it wasn't enough, so then we put in another 2. That was just right. So we'll do it again and put in 5.' They will estimate, when choosing a block to make a bridge, whether the block is a suitable length. Similarly, when loading up a truck, they will make decisions about how much it will hold, and whether they are strong enough to pull it when it is loaded, or if it is too heavy. They may set themselves a problem using a sand timer: 'Can I finish the jigsaw before all the sand runs through?' They can be encouraged to develop their problem-solving skills by:

- describing what they wish to do;
- choosing the materials for the task, using skills of estimation and approximation, and refining their choice as they work;
- carrying out their plan, with adult intervention to discuss how closely their plan

fits their original planning, and the reasons for changes made;

- reviewing the completed task, describing its features, and checking whether what they have produced is fit for the purpose;
- using appropriately the language of measures in their discussions.

Concept map (Table 5.1)

This shows the concepts outlined above in matrix form. Some example activities are shown so that the map can be used as a basis for planning. Some assessment checkpoints and key questions are given to show possible learning outcomes from the activities (and see Section 5.4).

5.3 Planning measuring experiences

Adult intervention in children's play

Children can be encouraged to explore measuring in their play. There will be opportunities to encourage estimation and approximation, and to make comparisons of lengths, weights and capacities. Many of the experiences which children will have of measures will come from their own choice of activities, such as deciding to dig a hole in the sandpit large enough to hold a pick-up truck. Here an adult can encourage children to make the estimate, and to use appropriate language in their questioning: Is the hole deep enough? How many spades of sand have you dug? Does the lorry fit in the hole?

Focused activities

Planned activities for developing concepts of measuring may include opportunities to develop across more than one aspect of measuring, rather than just concentrating upon one aspect. The following activities demonstrate both planning for a range of concepts, and activities which concentrate upon just one concept.

Teddies' tea party

An activity for four children:

- *Purpose:*   to make comparisons of size.
- *Materials:* four of each of these of different sizes: teddies, chairs, clothes for the teddies.
- *Language:* small, smaller, smallest, tall, long, full, empty, half . . .

How to begin

Each child chooses a teddy. They compare the teddies and by making direct comparisons put them in order of height. Ensure that they line the teddies up, with the feet in line. Ask:

- Which is the tallest teddy?
- Which is the shortest teddy?
- How can you tell?

Table 5.1 Concept map for measures

Key concept	Vocabulary	Examples of activities	Assessment checkpoints	Key questions
Use descriptive vocabulary	Big, little, long, short, thin, wide, tall, weigh, heavy, light, full, empty, cover, fit, big, little, large, small, tiny	Using blocks, construction kits; picking up parcels, using a balance, cooking; pouring and filling with sand, water, beads; putting the tablecloth onto the table; fitting items into a container; using descriptive vocabulary	• Uses descriptive vocabulary of size appropriately • Understands that different objects have differences of size	• Which is the big one? Why do you think that? • Can you find something about the same size as this?
Use comparative vocabulary	Longer, taller, shorter, wider, narrower, thicker, thinner, about the same, heavier, lighter, nearly, full, empty, more than, less than, cover, fit, too much, not enough, size, too big, too small	Dressing up; making models; pouring sand to balance a parcel; weighing out ingredients; pouring drinks at snack time; pouring and filling in the water or sand tray; finding a sheet of paper large enough to cover a box; fitting lids to saucepans; putting away the blocks by matching them to their outline drawn on paper; using comparative vocabulary	• Uses descriptive vocabulary of size appropriately • Uses opposites to compare sizes	• Can you put these in order of size? Which is the bigger . . .? How did you decide how to do it?
Make ordered arrangements	Longest, tallest, shortest, widest, heaviest, lightest, about the same, most, least, nearly, full to the top, half full, empty	Putting ribbons, pencils, scarves, in order of length; piling up the parcels for the postman, with the heaviest at the bottom, the lightest at the top; finding the cup which holds the most, the one that holds the least; using superlative vocabulary	• Puts items in order of size • Uses superlative vocabulary appropriately • Makes estimations and approximations • Uses measuring equipment appropriately	• Can you put these in order? Which is the tallest? How did you decide how to do it? • How much do you think this holds? How can you find out how much it holds?

Table 5.1 (continued)

Sequence events	Today, yesterday, tomorrow, morning, afternoon, next, before, after, then, now, days of the week, weekend . . .	Sequencing photographs, pictures in event order; recalling events in order; predicting what will happen next; changing the daily calendar; marking off the days on a count-down calendar . . .	• Puts events in time order • Uses vocabulary of time appropriately • Recalls events of significance • Makes reasonable predictions of the future	• What do you think will happen next? Why do you think that? What else might happen? • What do we do next?
Experience different rates of speed	Stop, go, slow, slowly, slowest, fast, quick . . .	Using musical instruments, moving toys, things that drip, own movements, to show differences in speed	• Can change tempo of own movements • Uses vocabulary of speed to describe changes in tempo	• Which moved fastest? How do you know that? Which do you think will go the slowest? How can we find out?
Compare different units of time	Days of the week; the months, o'clock times, minutes, hours, days . . .	Turning the hands on clocks; observing and using sand timers, rocker timers, water clocks	• Uses vocabulary of time appropriately	• What day is it today? What day will it be tomorrow? • What can we do before the sand runs out of the timer? What else could we try?
Use developing mathematical ideas and methods to solve practical problems	Pattern, puzzle; What could we try next? How did you work it out?	Making a tower as tall as themselves; finding which is the heaviest parcel; finding two containers which hold about the same amount; using a sand timer to see what they can do before the sand runs through	• Explains the plan and describes what was done • Uses appropriate measures vocabulary to explain	• What other materials could you use? • How could you make this even better? • How did you work it out? • What could we try next?

- What happens when I stand this teddy on the chair? Is this one still the tallest?
- Which one is higher than this one?

The children choose a chair for their teddy. Ask them to explain how they have decided which chair each teddy has. Accept their responses, and, if they have not done so, encourage them to think about ordering the chairs by size and placing the teddies on them according to teddy height.

Extend the activity by asking the children to choose suitable clothes for the teddies and asking them how they sorted the clothes.

Baking
An activity for four children:

- *Purpose:*   to experience balancing.
- *Materials:*   self-raising flour, eggs, soft margarine, castor sugar, balance, bowls, wooden spoons, paper cake-cases, bun tin, oven temperature 180°C.
- *Language:*   weigh, balance, more, less, about the same, enough, heavier, lighter . . .

How to begin
Encourage the children to hold the unbroken egg carefully and to feel how heavy it is. They can compare its weight to other things, and decide whether it feels heavier or lighter than those. Then the children take turns to balance their egg, still in its shell, with flour, then margarine, then sugar, putting the ingredients into the bowl each time. Ask:

- How much flour do you think we'll need?
- Is there enough yet? How can you tell?
- What happens if we pour some more?

When the children have weighed out their ingredients, the egg is broken into the bowl and the mixture beaten to make cake batter. The cakes are baked in the usual way.

Instead of using the egg to balance the other ingredients, a dial scale, or a balance with metric weights, can be used to weigh out ingredients for a recipe. With a dial scale children observe the pointer to find the given weight. Using metric weights and a balance, encourage children to feel the weight first, before pouring out the ingredients.

Snack-time drinks
An activity for a group of children (Figure 5.8):

- *Purpose:*   to make fair shares of liquid.
- *Materials:*   snack time drink, large jug, identical beakers for each child, with straight sides and an elastic band on the beaker.
- *Language:*   pour, enough, more, less, empty, full, half full.

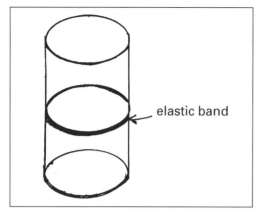

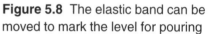

Figure 5.8 The elastic band can be moved to mark the level for pouring

How to begin

Discuss with the children how much of the drink they think they can each have so that everyone has the same. Talk about fair shares, where everyone has an identical beaker with about the same amount of the drink. The children move their elastic band so that it marks a point of more than half full and then compare where they have marked. Pass the jug around the group so that everyone has a turn at pouring. Ask:

- Do all the beakers have the same amount? How can we tell?
- What happens if we fill the beaker right to the top? (It will spill!)
- There is some drink left. How many more beakers can we fill like these? Let's pour and see if we made a good guess.

Ask the children to move the elastic band to about half full, then drink some and see if they have half a beaker of drink left. Ask if they made a good guess for half full. Then ask them to drink until their beakers are empty.

The elastic bands can be moved up and down the beakers to mark the filling point and for marking estimates. Instead of using drinks at snack time, water coloured with food dye can be used.

Making models

An activity for four children:

- *Purpose:* to compare models with the same volume.
- *Materials:* interlocking cubes, small boxes.
- *Language:* size, same, big, bigger, biggest, larger, smaller, different . . .

How to begin

Children choose some cubes and make a staircase. Ask them to compare their staircases. Ask if they have all used the same number of cubes. Ask them to choose the same number of cubes again and make a different model. Ask:

- Whose model is the biggest/smallest? How do you know?

- Which models used the same number of cubes?

Each child chooses a box and packs their cubes into it. Ask if they can find a different way to pack the cubes.

As an extension, children make models using five cubes each time. Ask them to make different models. Discuss how the models all have different shapes, but use five cubes each time, that is, they are the same size.

Recalling a special event
An activity for all the children at circle time.

- *Purpose:*   to sequence events.
- *Materials:*   large photographs of a very recent special event.
- *Language:*   before, next, after, then, now . . .

How to begin
With the children sitting in a circle, so that all will be able to see the photographs, show them one photo and ask what was happening. Encourage children to recall the events of that day. They can explain:

- Why the day was so special.
- Who any special visitors were and why they came.
- If it was an outing, where everyone went and how they got there.

Show the photographs. Ask individuals to come out and hold the photos so that everyone can see them. Then ask which photo shows the first part of that special day, and the next and so on, until they are in event order.

Children can take it in turns to tell the story of the day, using the photos to remind them of what happened. The photographs can be mounted in sequence as a display, or placed in an album, which children use to remind themselves of what happened.

Rocker timers
An activity for four children:

- *Purpose:*   to mark the passage of time.
- *Materials:*   coffee jar lids, card, glue, felt pens or crayons, plasticine.
- *Language:*   slow, slowly, slowest, quickly, about the same, more, less . . .

How to begin
Help the children to cut out a piece of card to fit the coffee lid, with a triangular extension to fit above the lid (Figure 5.9).

Figure 5.9 To make a rocker timer: put a lump of Plasticine at the base of a coffee jar lid, then stick a piece of card to the front of the lid

The children can decorate their piece of card, making a clown, Father Christmas, or patterned decoration. They stick the card to the front of the lid and place a small piece of plasticine at the base of the back of the lid. When the glue has dried the rocker timer is ready for use.

Show the children how to set the timer rocking, by pulling down on the point until it touches the table, then let go. Ask:

- Which timer rocks for the longest/shortest time?
- Can you put all the felt pens back in the box before the timer stops?
- What do you think you can do which lasts for a longer/shorter time than the timer?

The children can order their timers, from shortest to longest lasting. They can use their timers to time short activities, such as:

- building a tower until the timer stops;
- see how many shells they can put into a box;
- see how much clearing up can be done;
- see if there is time to write their name.

Alternatively, children can use commercially available timers, such as sand, water and rocker timers, which they set going, and then try to finish a short activity before the timer is finished.

Involving adult helpers in the planned activities

The skills of measuring and the associated language are used in everyday life. This language should be used correctly and in appropriate contexts and can be included on the weekly planning sheet so that all adults are aware of the language focus for the week. It is important to use the language of time in such a way that children can make sense of it from their personal experience. References to, for example, a holiday still to come, should be linked to something within the child's experience, such as 'You see Grandma every Saturday. Three visits to Grandma, then it's holiday time.' There will be many incidental opportunities in the nursery to develop children's use of language for measures, such as dressing up and comparing the lengths of the clothes; seeing how much the guinea pig weighs and if he has become heavier; watching plants grow and marking a chart to show the growth each week. Recording for measures can include photographs, charts, and keeping a simple calendar which is changed every day to show the day and date. To ensure that all adults working in the nursery during that week are aware of any specific requirements with regard to language and recording, it is helpful to spend a few minutes before the start of each session agreeing the strategies to be adopted.

Measuring activities for nursery environments (Table 5.2)

Table 5.2 Measures activities for nursery environments

Environment	Concept/skill	Context
circle time	• compare and order heights • recognise changes of tempo • sequence days of the week	• playing lining up games: ordering heights • singing songs, playing instruments: slowly, faster . . . • changing the calendar; saying what day it is today, tomorrow . . .
art and craft areas	• compare and order lengths, widths, sizes, areas	• making dough models: making a longer, fatter, wider worm • painting wider, shorter lines • covering a box with paper • making models: larger, smaller, taller . . .
table-top games and collections	• compare volumes, capacities • compare timing devices	• fitting beads, buttons, cotton reels, shells into boxes • ordering nesting and stacking toys • using sand, water, rocker timers
sand and water play	• compare and order capacities and volumes • explore balancing • explore rates of speed	• making sand pies in size order • filling and pouring sand and water; estimating • how many cups can be filled from a container • using a colander to separate larger items from the sand • using a bucket balance with sand or water play • watching how quickly water pours through tubing; making it go faster, more slowly
construction	• compare and order length • explore rates of speed	• making models: comparing to find longer, shorter, taller . . . • running cars down slopes • finding who finishes building their tower first • using a timing device when making a model • taking apart old clocks; turning the hands; as part of a 'clock repair shop'
block play	• compare and order length	• making models: estimating which pieces will fit; making a roadway longer, shorter, wider, to go from the cupboard to the door . . .

Table 5.2 (continued)

role play	• compare and order length, weight, capacity, sizes • use the language of time	• dressing up: wearing a longer dress, scarf, smaller shoes, longer cloak • sharing out drinks in the café • weighing the dolls at the chemist • using a clock in the home area
miniworlds	• compare and order sizes	• ordering the play people by height • ordering the cars by length • putting all the large animals in one field, the small ones in another
outside play	• explore rates of speed	• using moving toys and vehicles to move more slowly, more quickly • running races, finding who finished first
cooking	• explore weighing and pouring	• weighing out ingredients • balancing ingredients • pouring out spoonfuls, jugfuls
information technology	• compare and order lengths	• using art software to draw larger, smaller, longer, wider lines and pictures
music table	• use different tempos	• playing instruments slowly, quickly, getting faster, getting slower

5.4 Assessment

Observing children while they work, encouraging them to discuss what they are doing, and asking them to review what they have done, will give insights into their understanding of concepts of measurement. Use the assessment checkpoints and key questions in Table 5.1 to help with assessment. Where evidence of achievement in a standard form is required, the observational evidence can be supported by a note of the assessment checkpoint, with date and comment attached to show when the evidence of achievement was noted. This may identify whether children can:

- use descriptive language for length, weight, capacity, area and volume;
- use comparative language when comparing two or more objects; use opposites appropriately;
- make ordered arrangements of length, capacity and weight;
- sequence events; recognise that there were events that happened in the past and that there will be things happening in the future; use language of time, such as days of the week;
- experience different rates of speed, such as running, walking slowly, playing musical instruments;
- compare different units of time, and explore the use of simple timing devices.

Opportunities to make such assessments may occur incidentally during children's chosen activity or through specifically targeted focused activity.

Children respond well to questions such as:

- Can you put these in order of size?
- Which is the bigger . . .?

especially where they have been encouraged to respond using the mathematical vocabulary that they hear the adults using. Gradually they begin to respond in sentences and this should be encouraged.

What three and four year olds find more difficult are questions which ask 'How do you know?' such as:

- How did you decide how to do it?

Here the children tend not to respond. PGCE students trialled some of the key questions in 2001 and discovered that young children did not cope well with this sort of question. However, with practice, and with examples of how they might answer given by adults, they do begin to answer the 'How do you know?' type of question in a satisfactory way.

Possible errors in concepts and skills of measuring

Children's understanding and use of measuring will be limited by their ability to make direct comparisons and to conserve; these are concepts which will be developed when they are older. Early misunderstandings include:

- *Length.* Not comparing both ends of an object with both ends of another. To overcome this, it is helpful to ask children to place one end of each of the objects to be compared in line so that the other ends can be compared for differences in length. Children at this stage are unlikely to use a stick or tape to make a comparison. They have not yet understood that a mark can be made on a stick to represent a given length.
- *Capacity.* Pouring from one container to another; where the level appears higher up the container, the children will believe that this container contains more water. Even when they pour all the water back into the original container they are not convinced. This is because children do not conserve the capacity of the container nor the volume of liquid in it.
- *Weight.* Large parcels will be regarded as heavy; small parcels as light. Children will need encouragement to pick up and compare a wide range of sizes, shapes and weights of parcels before they begin to understand that the visual image does not reflect the weight.
- *Sequencing time events.* Children find the notions of past and future far more difficult to understand than the present. Often language of time is misused, so that past events were 'yesterday', and future events may all be 'tomorrow'. Some children, whose second language is English, may not have words in their home language for describing past and present, so that such concepts will not be explored in the same way at home.
- *The passing of time.* Children may begin to recognise special clock times, such as noon or home time. They will not be able to tell the time for some years yet.

They will not yet see that two different speeds can be compared, and will assign the results of two different speeds to other factors, such as effort.

These misunderstandings are to do with developmental processes and children will understand these concepts in time. Further experiences of the concepts, and opportunities to explore materials, will enable children to begin to build their schemas for these concepts to enhance their understanding.

5.5 Working in partnership with parents and carers

At home, children will hear the language of measures used in many different contexts. They will see their parents making comparisons, such as Have the curtains shrunk?, How heavy is the new baby now?, How long will the car journey take? They will be aware that clocks are set for recording video programmes and that the alarm clock wakes everyone in the morning. Thus, both at home and at nursery, they will hear this rich language used in a variety of contexts.

Activities at home for developing understanding of measuring

These activities do not require any special equipment as they make use of everyday items in the home.

Length
- *At home:* completing a growth chart on a regular basis for all the children; making cheese straws (long ones, short ones, wide ones); making paper chains at Christmas to go right across the room.
- *In the park:* finding the tallest tree, the shorter path; finding who can jump the furthest.
- *Shopping:* finding the longest cucumber; finding a dress or pair of trousers which is just long enough; measuring height on the shop's height chart; buying a new pair of shoes that are long enough.

Capacity
- *In the bath:* filling up the bath, watching the water level rise; making bubbles; using squeezy toys in the bath; filling up containers until they sink.
- *In the kitchen:* helping with the washing up; talking about water levels; pouring out drinks and talking about how much.
- *Shopping:* looking at the different shaped bottles which hold one litre; watching the meter turn as the petrol tank is filled.

Weight
- *At home:* weighing out ingredients for cooking; using the bathroom scales; comparing by lifting the weights of different food packets.
- *Shopping:* observing items being weighed; helping to put items into the bag and weighing them at a serve-yourself counter.
- *Health clinic:* watching how the babies are weighed.

Sequencing events

- *Recall:* recalling a story in order; recalling an exciting event in order; remembering the sequence of the day; looking at the family photograph album and talking about the people and events.
- *Predicting:* what will happen next; what will we do next week; deciding on what to do to celebrate a birthday.

The passing of time

- *Clocks:* finding the different types of clock in the house: video timer, cooker timer, wall clock, digital watch . . .; looking for clocks when at the shops; watching the hands move on a watch; watching the numerals change on a digital watch; knowing when it is time to go to bed.
- *Timing events:* helping to set the video timer; setting the kitchen timer; winding up an old-fashioned clock.
- *Time words:* using the days of the week; recognising the changes in season, special celebrations which mark the year.

CHAPTER 6

Planning, Organising and Assessing for Mathematics

6.1 The importance of play

Play is a key element in young children's learning. It is through play that they explore social interactions, learning about turn-taking, discussion and sharing (Sheridan, 1977) and explore mathematical concepts. Children's play is developmental; solitary, parallel and collaborative play are normally seen as a sequential development (Bunker *et al.*, 1982). Adults working in the nursery help children through these stages of development to encourage collaboration in planning what to do, implementing the plan, and discussing the outcomes, thus sharing understanding of mathematical concepts and using mathematical skills in purposeful group activity.

- *Solitary play:* one child, playing alone, without reference to others. This form of play begins early in life, for example when a baby plays with her toes, and continues throughout life, whenever a child, or an adult, wishes to take part in a solitary activity. In the nursery a child may play with a doll, complete a jigsaw puzzle, or make a painting.
- *Parallel play:* playing with the same materials as others, but not communicating. Two children may be sitting at the same table, making plasticine models. They will be engaged in similar activities but do not discuss what they are doing, or use each other's ideas.
- *Collaborative play:* this involves a common activity, sharing materials and discussing the activity. An example of this is children working with the blocks, making a roadway for cars. They discuss the size of their model, the layout, whether the cars will fit on the road, and work together to a common purpose.

It is through both structured play activities, where an adult has clear learning outcomes in mind, and activities where children have planned for themselves, that mathematical learning takes place. It should be noted that in both instances planning is involved: either that of the adult, or that of the child. The adult's role in both types of activities is crucial, as the adult will introduce and use new language, and encourage discussion to help the child to understand a concept or acquire a skill.

6.2 Equality of opportunity

Mathematical opportunities occur in all nursery environments. Children can explore numbers and counting, shapes, and movement, compare sizes and make patterns, whilst working in the home area, building constructions with blocks, or making models in the sandpit. Children will have preferences for what they wish to do. Some children may not choose to work in every environment, and so may risk not having a full range of experiences. There is evidence (Sheridan, 1977; Ross and Browne, 1993) that children perceive activities in a gender-related way, so that some children may regard particular toys or environments as 'boys' toys' or 'girls' toys' and avoid them. There may be adult beliefs which suggest that particular toys or activities have a gender bias, for example, that boys spend more time with construction toys and produce more complex models than girls. Walden and Walkerdine (1982) found that there was no difference in boys' and girls' abilities to manipulate materials, yet still such attitudes may persist. For children from ethnic minorities there may be issues of language and culture for adults to consider. It may be that a child's home language does not have equivalent vocabulary for some mathematical concepts, such as time concepts of tomorrow and yesterday, and this would suggest that adults would benefit from having some knowledge of the children's culture and beliefs, especially where there are differences from those of the adults. Adults in the nursery must be aware of children's choices of activities, and the learning opportunities that these provide (Dowling, 1988). From the full range of quality activities offered over time, adults will be able to offer all children access to the full range of mathematical concepts and skills.

In order to ascertain the use of provision by individual children, a simple observation checklist may provide useful information. The following which was originally developed for technology by Ross and Browne (1993) is here adapted for mathematical learning.

- the range of activities/environments which children choose;
- how children use the materials provided or chosen;
- how often individual children return to a specific environment or activity;
- which activities or environments are dominated by particular children or groups of children;
- the type of play which activities or environments encourage: solitary, parallel, collaborative;
- whether there appears to be gender bias in any activity or environment.

From such observations any bias in individual children's choice of type of activity will be identified, and children can be encouraged to access the range of mathematical opportunities available to them.

6.3 Planning

The contribution of this book to planning

Each chapter contains a discussion of theoretical considerations of child development and mathematical development. Key concepts and skills are discussed in detail, with examples of planned activities. There are concept maps for each of the mathematical topics which show the key concepts, the language development, example activities and assessment checkpoints. For each mathematical topic there is a checklist for the nursery environment showing the environments, concepts and skills which can be developed, and sample activities. All of these elements are helpful in the planning process.

Identifying mathematics concepts and skills in topics from the chapters

The maps and checklists in each chapter can be used as planning tools, as they give the basic ingredients for planning specific mathematical activities. From these resources, planning can be undertaken as follows:

- *Long-term planning:* for a cycle of one, two or three years, depending upon how long children normally attend the nursery. This shows the range of mathematical concepts across all the topic areas of number, pattern, shape and measures, and how these will be covered in the given period.
- *Medium-term planning:* for about a month to six weeks. This may be based on themes, such as 'Toys' or 'Summer', but within it the mathematical content is clear and the concepts and skills to be developed are identified.
- *Short-term planning:* for a week, and on a daily basis. The weekly plan identifies how individual environments will contribute to the mathematical concepts to be developed, and includes specific structured activities. Details of resources needed and language development will help all adults to be aware of what the provision should encompass. The daily plan shows individual responsibilities for both routine tasks, with any mathematics to be drawn from these, and specific focused teaching. Whether the focused teaching is intended for all or for specific groups, on a rota basis through the day or week, needs to be clarified in the plan.

Mathematical learning will not just happen; careful planning is needed to ensure that opportunities for developing understanding of specific concepts are offered. The choice of materials in each environment will need to be considered carefully, so that these reflect the learning outcomes identified in the planning. It would be impractical to resource each environment to develop a particular concept or skill; however, it is helpful to be aware of ways in which the concept can be developed incidentally and it is likely that such opportunities will arise at any time. Table 6.1 shows the planning for an aspect of counting (see Chapter 1).

Table 6.1 An example of a weekly planning sheet

2nd–6th June			
Concept	Activities	Resources	Assessment
Count items which can be partitioned (moved) Language counting numbers one, two, three . . . the same, different, enough, more, not enough, too many, nearly the same . . .	Counting how many by touching and moving Table top beads on laces; pegs on a pegboard; magnetic shape tiles. Miniworlds cars and garage; playbus and people. Baker's Shop pennies in purses; breads and cakes on the shelves. Collage counting items for butterfly collage	Table top beads, laces; pegs and pegboards; magnetic shape tiles, boards Miniworlds cars, garage, road; playbus and people Shop pennies, purses, shopping bags, clay cakes and breads Collage pasta spirals, shells, large sequins, glue, glue spreaders	Does the child ● count each item only once? ● coordinate the count with the partition?

Planning for progression and continuity

In each of the chapters a progression for the mathematical topic is shown and this can, on entry to school, be mapped into any of the National Curricula for the United Kingdom. Children of three and four have fairly short concentration spans and so will probably spend the greater part of their time in nursery in activities of their own choice. It is therefore vitally important to ensure that planned activity builds upon children's current understanding and that sufficient time for development, through a cycle of returning to a topic, is given.

Balance between aspects of mathematics topics needs to be considered when planning. Counting and Number will be a feature of each day in the nursery, through counting rhymes, putting out and putting away items, or children deciding how many cars or play people they need. Shape and Space, Measures and Pattern activities will be going on during the week, through children's choice, but adults may not be so aware of this unless it has been specifically planned or they join in the children's play. The planning cycle must take account of all the aspects of mathematics and the adults need to decide upon a suitable balance of provision, across the topics.

Language

In each chapter vocabulary associated with the concept is given. It is essential, as has been stated elsewhere in this book, that adults use language correctly, so that children develop understanding of new vocabulary, how it is used, and the contexts in which it is used. It is suggested that when planning focused activities, where adults plan to be involved in the children's learning, the language to be used is decided beforehand. The adults will think through, before the activity, what language they will use and how it will be used, and thus be prepared to extend children's understanding through careful questioning.

Mathematical language can be introduced through incidental occurrences, such as through reading a story where the mathematical content is strong. Both fiction and non-fiction books can be used. However, the book must be meaningful to the children and the mathematical connections natural (Thatcher, 2001). Books give opportunities to ask What if . . .? questions where children can use both their imaginations and their knowledge in order to think about what might happen next.

Focused activities

Where there are both three and four year olds in the nursery, with their differing developmental needs, planning needs to take account of this through differentiation. Children may be grouped by age and learning achievement so that carefully structured and targeted teaching takes place. For example, those children who need more experience of counting can work with adults on specifically planned activities to help them to develop their skills, whilst others whose counting skills are more developed may be involved in different number-based activities, building upon their knowledge and understanding. Children need to know the purpose of the activity and the adult's intentions, so that the children understand what is expected of them and, through discussion with the adult, can reflect upon their achievement.

Interactions in children's play

For most children how they spend the majority of their time in the nursery will be determined by their own choice. They will choose where to play, what to do, whether to work with others or to work alone. Whilst some of the environments may contain specific materials placed there by an adult to encourage exploration of particular concepts and skills, other environments will have a range of materials from which the children make a free choice. Interactions in children's play cannot be planned by adults; they will arise from children's choice of activities, and their questions and comments. However, adults need to be aware of the mathematical possibilities within each environment, whether specifically resourced or not, as the quality of interaction depends upon the adult's understanding of the mathematical concepts, so that appropriate questioning skills and language are used. This approach will encourage the child's further understanding of the concept and help them to reflect upon their learning, so that they are aware of what they have learnt and how that is useful to them.

Role of adults

All the adults working in the nursery need to be aware of the mathematics teaching focus. During the planning meeting, it is helpful to agree the range of language to be developed. Where parents or carers work in the nursery for a short period of time, they should be aware of the focus for the week. A daily plan is useful, as this can be used to show what each adult's role will be for the day and can also act as a reminder about the appropriate use of new or specific mathematical vocabulary.

Table 6.2 An example of a daily planning sheet

Monday 2nd June	
9am	Welcome children into the nursery.
	Jill: book area
	Zena: table top area: lacing beads, counting how many by moving beads along the lace.
	Mary: craft table: making a butterfly collage on drawn butterfly shapes, using pasta shapes and large sequins. Children count out matching quantities for each side of the butterfly. Count by touching and moving.
	June: outside
	Margaret (parent helper): please would you choose three or four children to help to prepare snacks and drinks. Raisins, milk and squash.
9.40	Clearing up.
9.50	Into main hall for movement session.
10.10	Into groups. Registers. Snack time: counting out five raisins each.
10.30	Focus activity for Jill's and Zena's groups in Rainbow Room: counting farm animals by touching and moving.
	Margaret: table top area: snap card game.
	Mary: outside: feeding the pets.
	June: outside: by the climbing equipment.
11.10	Clearing up.
	Jill: Circle time. Counting rhymes: Peter hammers with one hammer; One elephant went out to play. Story: The three bears.

It is more difficult to ensure that volunteers are confident in their mathematical ability, but a daily plan which all adults including volunteers are expected to refer to will help to raise awareness of the purpose of activities. However, whilst the majority of parents in a recent study, which looked at parents' roles and the education of their children, recognised that they had a positive and important role to play, they felt themselves to be deskilled when it came to helping within the school environment (Caddell *et al.*, 2000). Where possible, including volunteers in planning and evaluation discussions will raise their awareness of the mathematical issues in the chosen topics and successful ways of tackling them.

Record of activities

The planned focused teaching activities which individual children have experienced need to be recorded so that, over time, there is a record of their experiences (Table 6.3). This will show who has explored which concepts and skills and can be used in conjunction with assessment records for forward planning to make decisions about individual children's learning needs. It is helpful if the record shows concepts, skills, the activities and dates. Such a record can be for individual children or groups and can be part of what is passed on to the receiving school.

A record, such as the above, can be completed on a weekly basis, to show what has been undertaken, with the activities briefly indicated. This is not a record of achievement, but of entitlement and experience. It gives no indication of what has been understood and is not intended to do so. It is useful as it shows the experiences and omissions for individuals. Where there is both full- and part-time attendance, this record is essential. It will help adults to plan for breadth of experience and for progression.

Organisation

Children who need encouragement to become more autonomous will benefit from being encouraged to make decisions about what they wish to do and from choosing the materials they will need. Children's understanding of mathematical concepts can be enhanced through their ability to access materials and environments:

- Clear labelling of shelves, so that children can find what they need. An outline drawn on shelf paper which matches the outline of boxed games will help children to put them away again, and give them experience in matching sizes, through matching the shape of the bottom of the box with its outline.
- Outlines of sand and water materials, on shelf paper, or on pegboards. Children can hang sieves onto the pegs to fit the outline shape, and put buckets onto their outlines on a shelf.
- Blocks stored by shape and size. Where there is room, a section of wall can be marked with block outlines, so that the blocks can be put back, matching them to their shape and size outline.
- Name tags which hang from a board for all children. Children take their name tag and place it on a board in the area where they have chosen to work. Where

Table 6.3 Record of experiences

Topic	Key Concept	Experience/Date
Counting	<ul><li>Use language of quantity to make comparisons, such as more, the same.</li><li>Consistently recite the number names in order.</li><li>Count items which can be partitioned (moved).</li><li>Count the same set again, with the items in a different order/ array.</li><li>Count items which can be touched but not moved (items in a picture).</li><li>Count items which can be seen but not touched.</li><li>Count sounds.</li><li>Count physical movements.</li><li>Count out a given quantity of items.</li><li>Use developing mathematical ideas and methods to solve practical problems.</li></ul>	
Number	<ul><li>Begin to use the language of ordering.</li><li>Know that $N+1$ is one more than N and $N-1$ is one fewer than N.</li><li>Develop strategies such as finger counting, mental imagery, for addition and subtraction of small quantities.</li><li>Begin to make reasonable estimates of small quantities.</li><li>Recognise and use appropriate language to describe zero, both cardinal and ordinal aspects.</li><li>Make fair shares of a quantity.</li><li>Use language of division, and fractions.</li><li>Name some larger numbers.</li><li>Recognise contexts where larger numbers are used.</li><li>Make a record of numbers, using a pictographic, iconic or symbolic response.</li><li>Name some numerals.</li><li>Use developing mathematical ideas and methods to solve practical problems.</li></ul>	
Pattern	<ul><li>Describe an order.</li><li>Describe and make line patterns.</li><li>Copy a sequence.</li><li>Create a sequence.</li><li>Create a pattern.</li><li>Recognise cyclic patterns.</li><li>Use developing mathematical ideas and methods to solve practical problems.</li></ul>	
Shape and Space	<ul><li>Describe natural and manufactured shapes.</li><li>Construct and deconstruct shapes by fitting together, taking apart, rearranging and reshaping.</li><li>Simple properties of 3D shapes.</li><li>Lines: patterns and directions.</li><li>Simple properties of 2D shapes.</li><li>Reflection and symmetry.</li><li>Position and movement.</li><li>Interpret pictorial representations of spatial relationships.</li><li>Use developing mathematical ideas and methods to solve practical problems.</li></ul>	
Measures	<ul><li>Use descriptive language.</li><li>Use comparative language.</li><li>Make ordered arrangements.</li><li>Sequence events.</li><li>Experience different rates of speed.</li><li>Compare different units of time.</li><li>Use developing mathematical ideas and methods to solve practical problems.</li></ul>	

there is a number limit, for example, four children to work in the sand, the children can check whether there is a spare peg for their tag, or count how many tags are already hanging on the board. This gives opportunities for interpreting data such as 'how many', 'how many more' and 'who' are working in specific areas.

- Clearing-up time offers excellent opportunities for sorting by given criteria and for matching by shape and size. Where materials are stored by colour or by type, the red tea set, the blue set of cutlery . . . then children can sort by colour. Materials can be sorted by shape, with the round beads in one box and the cuboid ones in another. Stacking and nesting toys will be ordered by size so that they can be put away. Inset jigsaws will need to be completed before being put away, so that children will match shapes and sizes to the outlines. Time to clear away properly is important, as it will offer children opportunities to use their growing skills in sorting and matching.

Case studies on planning

These two case studies show two different approaches to planning. In the first the planning for mathematical learning began, at least in the eyes of the teacher-in-charge, from the Early Learning Goals of the Foundation Stage Curriculum, and the planning for mathematical learning was rigorous and included both focused activities and awareness of opportunities which might arise from the child's choice during the day. The second nursery planned with great care, starting from a term's topic, then fitting the chosen activities to the Early Learning Goals of the Foundation Stage Curriculum. In both cases the planning was structured, but the starting points were different, and for the second nursery it could be assumed that planning for progression and continuity in mathematics learning might be lost. The first example shows a very structured approach to planning. This may be too structured for some; however, in practice the children had freedom to follow their own interests for part of each session. In the second example the structure is looser, but the adults took advantage of opportunities to extend understanding.

Planning in a nursery unit attached to a primary school

In the nursery unit there were a qualified teacher, and a nursery nurse, with help from parents. The children attended for five half days per week. The teacher-in-charge led the team of adults. Before the children began at the nursery there was a home visit from the teacher who took with her a prospectus, explained to the parents how the nursery operated and also brought a photo album of activities to show what went on. This visit occurred in the week before the child started at the nursery. This gave the teacher insights into the child's needs as an aid for future planning and also helped the child and parents to have some ideas about what happened in the nursery.

Planning was undertaken by the teacher and the nursery nurse, with time built in for this into the nursery nurse's contract. The planning started from the Early

Learning Goals of the Foundation Stage Curriculum, and the teacher had a clear view of what needed to be covered. They also used themes which were planned across the curriculum. They planned at three levels for each area of learning. For mathematics:

- *Long-term planning:* this was a basic outline which identified the aims for a term or half term, such as: 'to develop and use mathematical language and develop simple mathematical ideas: positional vocabulary (experienced through weaving, outdoor play in dens and tunnels, music using "Bear Hunt", 3D display table where things go in/under/through etc., in shop, travel agents for money)'. Themes were also identified.
- *Medium-term planning:* here the Early Learning Goals coverage was identified, within the chosen theme. The teacher ensured that there was continuity and progression within the planning and that the range of abilities were met, as shown through the Stepping Stones in the Foundation Stage Curriculum. Also, it was decided how to set up the environments in order to meet the planning requirements and to support the theme.
- *Daily planning:* this was completed for a week at a time and would include both the specific goal, written as a Key Objective, and contexts taken from the Stepping Stones examples of what the children do and what the practitioner needs to do.

However, after some thought the nursery nurse pointed out that she had always assumed that the planning came from the theme and that the Early Learning Goal links were added subsequently. The teacher-in-charge commented that she could only assume that this was because the nursery nurse was used to planning starting from the themes, and that she, the teacher, always had the Early Learning Goals firmly in mind as they planned.

Each week at least one focused activity for mathematics was planned. This was an activity which was planned with an adult in attendance with the children, who was aware of the purpose of the activity, the resources to be used and their purpose and the language to be developed. Each week the parent helper was informed of the planning for their next time in the nursery, then reminded on the day of what had been planned.

At first a letter had been sent home to parents on a weekly basis to inform them of what the planning was for the next week, but it was impossible to continue with this due to insufficient administration time. Instead a notice would be put on the parents' board about every three weeks informing them of the theme and also which shape and number were being concentrated on. Parents were invited to come and help and to send in things which would help to support the theme. All parents were spoken to each day by one of the staff and photographic evidence was kept in the nursery to explain the activity.

Planning in a nursery school attached to a private preparatory school
At this nursery there were five staff and twenty-six children, aged two and a half to three and a half years. The nursery was led by a nursery nurse manager and the day could be much longer, from about 8 am to 6 pm if parents wanted this. Some children were brought to the nursery each day and collected by a nanny or mother's help, because both parents worked. The school was situated in an affluent area.

Time was provided for the staff team to meet together to plan. They chose a theme for a term, then brainstormed for activity ideas and made a spider plan which included the areas of the curriculum, such as Mathematical Development, Communication, Language and Literacy, to show how the areas of the curriculum were covered within the plan. To this the Early Learning Goal references were added. The plans included how the environments were to be resourced as well as the focused activities for each week, including that for mathematics.

A weekly plan was posted on the notice board so that staff knew what was planned on a weekly basis and also so that this was available for parents to inform them of what was planned. Parents did not come in to help within the nursery and it was staffed accordingly. However, parents and carers were spoken to each day and informed of the child's progress informally.

The staff relied upon OFSTED inspections to inform them of recent developments in nursery education. Very little in-service education was provided so that the staff relied upon their initial training to help them to provide a suitable learning environment.

Where planning is rigorous, and takes good account of the Early Learning Goals stages of development, children's learning is much more likely to show progression because it is possible to plan for progression. Using a thematic approach, over time, all of the Early Learning Goals can be covered. However, these may not be covered systematically, in sufficient detail, or in such a way that the child can make sense of new concepts in the light of prior knowledge.

6.4 Assessment

Assessment of the child's mathematical knowledge, skills and understanding should identify significant achievements in the child's understanding and skill development. Assessment must

- be manageable;
- include the child in the evaluation process;
- enhance the learning and teaching process.

(adapted from Hutchin, 1996)

From the planning cycle (see section 6.3 above), mathematical topics and specific teaching and learning targets will be identified for all the children, groups or individuals. Similarly, assessment criteria need to be identified which relate to the learning targets. Within the Foundation Curriculum clear expectations are shown, through the Stepping Stones, of the children's stages of learning which lead to the Key Objectives from the National Numeracy Strategy Framework for the end of the reception year in school. Careful monitoring of the planning programme and of children's learning will show whether children are likely to attain the expected rate of progress, and this enables the adults in the nursery to adjust the planning according to need (Stephen and Wilkinson, 1999).

Significant achievement

It is significant achievement that needs to be identified and recorded in assessment. Significant achievement is something so important that it needs to be written down:

- it could be the first time that a child does or says something;
- it could be when an adult is sure that the child has thoroughly grasped a concept or skill;
- what is significant for one child may not be so for another.

Clarke and Atkinson (1996) identify the following categories of significant achievement; mathematical examples have been added:

- *Physical skill:* using a pencil or crayon in making tallies or writing numerals;
- *Social skill:* being able to take turns when playing a dice game;
- *Attitude development:* showing increased confidence in finding and putting away equipment;
- *Conceptual development:* counting each item in a set of toys just once and knowing that the last number in the count is the cardinal number of the set;
- *Process skill:* making a reasonable estimate of how many counters there are and checking by counting accurately.

Using assessment criteria

Table 6.3 shows key concepts, assessment criteria and key questions compiled from Chapters 1 to 5. They have been grouped under their mathematical topic and can be used to help to identify significant achievement.

Key questions

These are the questions that can be used to probe young children's understanding of the mathematical concepts. For each concept there are some suggested questions that can be used. These can be supplemented by other questions which encourage children to think mathematically and to answer using mathematical language. At first, young children will find it easier to answer questions of fact. By encouraging them to move from one word answers to sentences, then to answer questions where they need to describe what they did, or what they were thinking, they will become more fluent in their thinking and speaking about their mathematics. Three and four year olds find questions of the 'How did you know?' and 'What did you think?' type much more difficult to answer than those that are more factual, questions such as 'How many now?' and 'Are there more red or more blue?'

Table 6.4 Assessment criteria and key questions

Key concept	Assessment checkpoints	Key questions
Counting		
Use language of quantity to make comparisons, such as more, the same	• Responds appropriately to vocabulary • Uses vocabulary in context	• Have we enough? • How can you be sure that you have counted all of them? • Who has more/fewer? What if I have one more/fewer, now who has more/fewer?
Consistently recite the number names in order	• Recites the number names in order to five, ten, beyond ten to . . .	• Why do we have to say the number names in the same order when we count? • What would happen if we didn't start with one? • How can you be sure that you have counted all of them?
Count items which can be partitioned (moved)	• Counts each item only once • Coordinates the count with the partition	• How many did you count? How many . . . are there? • How many have you counted now? How many are there still to count? How do you know that?
Count the same set again, with the items in a different order/array	• Counts each item only once • Starts with a different item as 'one' • Counts same items in different arrays	• How many have you counted? • What if you started with . . . are there the same number? How do you know that? • What if you put them in a different group; how many now? How do you know?
Count items which can be touched but not moved (e.g. items in a picture)	• Counts each item • Counts each item only once	• How many are there? • How do you know you have counted them all?
Count items which can be seen but not touched	• Counts each item • Counts each item only once	• How many are there? • How do you know you have counted them all?
Count sounds	• Counts each sound • Counts each sound only once	• How many are there? • What if I tapped once more; how many then?
Count physical movements	• Coordinates movement with the count • Counts each move • Counts each move only once	• How many did you count? • (On a game board) Where did you start? How many did you count? Where did you land?
Count out a given quantity of items	• Counts out required number of items	• How many do you need? • How many did you count? • What if you need one more/fewer; how many then?

Table 6.4 (continued)

Use developing mathematical ideas and methods to solve practical problems	• Uses counting strategies to solve problems	• How many do you need? • How do you know that? • How did you work it out? • What could we try next?

Number

Begin to use the vocabulary of ordering	• Orders quantities • Uses vocabulary of order to describe position	• Who has more/most . . .? • What would you rather have: two cakes or four cakes? Why?
Know that N+1 is one more than N and N−1 is one fewer than N	• Knows how many for one more/fewer	• How many are there? (add/subtract one) Now how many are there?
Develop strategies such as finger counting, mental imagery, for addition and subtraction of small quantities	• Adds and subtracts small unseen quantities with reasonable accuracy	• I put three pennies in the money box, and now two more. How many are there? How do you know? • There are five people on the bus. I take out two. How many are left? How do you know?
Begin to relate addition to combining two groups of objects, and subtraction to 'taking away'	• Adds and subtracts using materials with reasonable accuracy	• There are some blue and red bricks here. Can you find a way of giving me seven bricks? How many red/blue are there? Can you find another way of doing this? • You have six bricks. If I took three how many would you have? How did you work it out?
Begin to make reasonable estimates of small quantities	• Estimates small quantities with reasonable accuracy • Subitises for small quantities	• How many do you think there are? How did you work that out?
Recognise and use appropriate vocabulary to describe zero, both cardinal and ordinal aspects	• Uses vocabulary of zero in context • Knows when there is nothing left • Counts down to zero	• How many are there? • If I put them all away, how many would there be on the table?
Make fair shares of a quantity	• Shares a quantity into equal groups • Recognises when a sharing is unfair	• Share these between us; how many do you have? How many do I have? Is that fair? • Now share these between the three dolls . . .
Use vocabulary of division and fractions	• Shares a quantity into equal groups • Recognises when a sharing is unfair • Cuts a whole into two similar (equal) pieces	• Share these between us; how many do you have? How many do I have? Is that fair? • Now share these between the three dolls . . . • How could you make this into two halves?

Table 6.4 (continued)

Name some larger numbers	● Names larger numbers in context	● What is your house number? ● Where can you find big numbers? ● How do you know that these are big numbers?
Recognise contexts where larger numbers are used	● Names larger numbers in context	● How much is that? ● What time is it? How do you know that?
Make a record of numbers, using a pictographic, iconic or symbolic response	● Records to show how many with reasonable accuracy ● Uses pictures, tallies or numerals to record quantities	● How many are there? ● (Of numerals) what number is that? ● Can you find me the number card to show how many there are?
Name some numerals and order them	● Reads some numerals accurately	● What number is that? ● Can you put these number cards in order for me? ● What comes next? ● What is between . . . and . . .? ● How do you know?
Use developing mathematical ideas and methods to solve practical problems	● Uses number-based strategies to solve problems	● How many do you think there are? ● How do you know that? ● How did you work it out? ● What could we try next?
Pattern		
Describe an order	● Identifies positions within the order, e.g. before, after ● Uses vocabulary of order appropriately	● What comes next/before/after? How do you know? ● Can you make a new pattern using these . . .?
Describe and make line patterns	● Describes the line shape ● Uses a range of lines to make patterns and designs	● Which shapes have you used? ● Can you make a different pattern using these lines?
Copy a sequence	● Copies a sequence accurately ● Identifies any differences	● Are these patterns the same? ● (Of a sequence with one piece different): Is this the same? What is different? Can you make these the same? How did you do that?
Create a sequence	● Uses imagination to make a sequence ● Describes the order	● Can you make a different pattern using the same pieces? ● How is it different? ● What will come next/between . . .?

Table 6.4 (continued)

Create a pattern	• Copies a sequence to make a pattern • Creates a sequence and copies it correctly to make a repeating pattern	• Can you make me a pattern where the second bead is red? Is there another way of doing that? • What will come next in your pattern?
Recognise cyclic patterns	• Describes a cyclic pattern • Finishes a cyclic pattern keeping repeats correct • Uses vocabulary of position and cyclic time	• What comes next? • Can you finish the pattern? • Tell me about your day: what did you do next? . . . and next?
Use developing mathematical ideas and methods to solve practical problems	• Makes patterns and describes them using appropriate vocabulary	• What other patterns could you make? • What other materials could you use to make that pattern? • How did you work it out? • What could we try next?

Shape and Space

Describe natural and manufactured shapes	• Sorts consistently for one/two property/ies • Uses vocabulary of texture, colour and feature appropriately • Describes similarities and differences	• Which group does this belong to? Why? How do you know? • What is the same about these? How are they different?
Construct and deconstruct shapes by fitting together, taking apart, rearranging and reshaping	• Fits pieces together and takes them apart • Makes and describes models using appropriate mathematical vocabulary • Plans what to make and how; revises plan to improve model	• Which pieces fit together? Can you make them fit together in a different way? • Can you make a different model with the same pieces? • How can you make your model better?
Simple properties of 3D shapes	• Uses shape vocabulary to describe properties • Uses movement vocabulary to describe properties of shapes	• Which shapes have flat/curved faces? • What could you make with these shapes? What else could you make? • Which shapes will roll? How could we find out?
Lines, patterns and directions	• Discriminates between line shapes and patterns • Uses shape and movement vocabulary to describe line patterns	• What patterns can you make in the sand? What other patterns could you make? What could you use to make them? • How could you make Roamer go over there?
Simple properties of 2D shapes	• Sorts consistently by properties of 2D shapes • Uses shape vocabulary to describe properties	• Describe this shape to a friend: can they guess what it is? • What shape will you see if you print with this?

Table 6.4 (continued)

Reflection and symmetry	• Uses flips and turns to find a fit • Uses vocabulary of reflection and symmetry to describe patterns, to describe patterns, pictures and shapes	• What can you see in the mirror? • (Blot and fold) What do you think you will see when you open up your paper? • Can you copy your partner's movements?
Position and movement	• Uses vocabulary of position and movement • Follows instructions which use position and movement vocabulary • Makes observations from different viewpoints	• What can you see? What do you think you will see if you look between your legs? • Where will you go if you move forward/sideways . . .? • How can we make Roamer go to the cupboard?
Interpret pictorial representations of spatial relationships	• Uses vocabulary of shape and position to describe objects in a picture • Observes/draws objects from different positions and identifies similarities and differences	• What can you see in the picture? Where is it? What is next to the . . .? • What if you draw it from over there? How will it look the same/different?
Use developing mathematical ideas and methods to solve practical problems	• Makes models or drawings and describes them using appropriate vocabulary • Moves from one place to another and describes what has been done	• What other models/pictures could you make? • What other materials could you use? • How could you make this even better? • How did you work it out? • What could we try next?

Measures

Use descriptive vocabulary	• Uses descriptive vocabulary of size appropriately • Understands that different objects have differences of size	• Which is the big one? Why do you think that? Can you find something about the same size as this?
Use comparative vocabulary	• Uses descriptive vocabulary of size appropriately • Uses opposites to compare sizes	• Can you put these in order of size? Which is the bigger . . .? How did you decide how to do it?
Make ordered arrangements	• Puts items in order of size • Uses superlative vocabulary appropriately • Makes estimations and approximations • Uses measuring equipment appropriately	• Can you put these in order? Which is the tallest? How did you decide how to do it? • How much do you think this holds? How can you find out how much it holds?
Sequence events	• Puts events in time order • Uses vocabulary of time appropriately • Recalls events of significance • Makes reasonable predictions of the future	• What do you think will happen next? Why do you think that? What else might happen? • What do we do next?

Table 6.4 (continued)

Experience different rates of speed	• Can change tempo of own movements • Uses vocabulary of speed to describe changes in tempo	• Which moved fastest? How do you know that? • Which do you think will go the slowest? How can we find out?
Compare different units of time	• Uses vocabulary of time appropriately	• What day is it today? What day will it be tomorrow? • What can we do before the sand runs out of the timer? What else could we try?
Use developing mathematical ideas and methods to solve practical problems	• Explains the plan and describes what was done • Uses appropriate measures vocabulary to explain	• What other materials could you use? • How could you make this even better? • How did you work it out? • What could we try next?

Problem-solving

As well as key concepts and assessment criteria for mathematical topics, skills in problem solving need to be considered and their acquisition assessed across a range of mathematical topics. As has been stated in each chapter of this book, problem-solving is an integral part of the nursery experience as children identify a problem, make a plan, implement it and then evaluate its effectiveness, or as nurseries which use High Scope strategies would say (Hohmann *et al.*, 1978):

- plan
- do
- recall

Problem-solving is embedded in the Foundation Curriculum as can be seen through the statement: 'Use developing mathematical ideas and methods to solve problems.' Children can be encouraged to develop their problem-solving skills through:

- identifying the problem and making a plan, either verbally or as a picture, or both;
- working at their plan, revising it as they go. Adults can help by asking open questions, such as 'What have you thought of so far?', 'What could you use to help you?' or 'What have you seen like this before?' (Early Childhood Mathematics Group, 1997);
- recalling what has been done. Children can discuss what they have made, or painted, or the solution to a problem, either with an adult or in a small group of children with an adult. They can develop their ability to use mathematical language and to ask and answer questions through discussion. Others can offer suggestions for improvement to the finished result.

Gary, four years three months, decided to make a 'car' from a cardboard box which he wore on shoulder straps over his body. He planned this carefully, talking it through with an adult, made a model from cardboard and at recall time was unhappy with his model.

Gary: It's too small. I think I need a bigger box.
Gemma: Longer straps.
Gary: I'll try that next.

The next day, Gary had three other children helping him. They made a new 'car', using a larger box and longer lengths of tape for the straps. All the children saw the finished 'car' at circle time and were very impressed. During the next few days most of the children made a car like Gary's for themselves.

In the Foundation Curriculum, the importance of problem-solving is recognised: 'They begin to use their developing mathematical understanding to solve practical problems.' The following assessment criteria will be helpful in identifying significant achievement in problem-solving processes:

- recognises which aspects of mathematics to use in the given context;
- makes and carries out a plan;
- evaluates the outcome and identifies possible improvements;
- has the confidence and motivation to complete the task, even when it proves difficult.

(adapted from Early Childhood Mathematics Group, 1997)

Using assessment as a formative process: making it manageable

As can be seen from Table 6.4, there are too many assessment criteria for each one to be assessed and to attempt to do so would lead to an impossible workload for adults. Instead, a matrix such as that in Table 6.4 has two functions:

- Guidance on what to look for in observation of children at work. The key concepts and assessment criteria for a specific topic can be identified and kept in mind for the duration of a mathematical topic. Adults will be able to keep these in mind and use them as a basis for their observation of individual children's significant achievement.
- A summative check of what needs to be covered. A record for each child, with the list of key concepts and assessment criteria, can be checked on a regular basis and highlighted and dated when there is evidence of significant achievement. Over a period of time, such a record will also highlight those children who are not making progress and those for whom little assessment has been undertaken.

Observation

Observation of children can occur during a focused activity and during a child's choice at play. What the child is doing and how and what they say during discussion may indicate significant achievement as may the child's response to open questions. The child will benefit from understanding that they have made a significant achievement and that this is to be recorded in their record. In order for there to be quality observation, adults must be aware of what the child has already achieved, which implies liaison between staff on a regular basis.

Outcomes

Once an assessment has been made and significant achievement acknowledged by the adult with the child, planning for the next stage of learning needs to be undertaken. Where children are grouped for focused teaching, the appropriateness of the planned teaching for those children needs to be reviewed. Those children who have not yet achieved will need to be given more help, perhaps during their own choice of activity. Those who have demonstrated their understanding will benefit from opportunities to use their understanding in problem-solving situations.

Recording significant achievement

It is important to record what has been observed at the time of the observation, or it may be forgotten. In some nurseries notebooks are used as children are observed, so that a brief note is made there and then. Others make a brief record on 'post-it' notes and the observation from the notes is written into the child's record at a later date. Sometimes conversations are taped, or photographs taken, perhaps of a model, or an adult may make a drawing of a child's model (Cubey, 1999). Sometimes a video record of nursery activities may be made. On a regular basis, the child's mathematical record of achievement needs to be cross-referenced with the assessment criteria (both for mathematical topics and for problem-solving processes) so that a full range of mathematical topics is explored by the child and the quality of learning assessed. In this way, following assessment, planning for the individual as well as the group will ensure children's entitlement to the breadth and depth of the mathematical curriculum.

Keeping records

There are three basic records which are needed. It is suggested that the records either are blocked into National Curriculum topics of Number (and counting), Pattern, Shape and Space, and Measures, as this will help the receiving school to match the individual child's achievement to school records, or reflect the Foundation Curriculum statements. The three basic records are:

- record of activities experienced;
- record of observations of significant achievement;
- record of assessment criteria, highlighted and dated to show understanding and skill development.

These three records can be enhanced by a portfolio of evidence containing samples of children's work or photographs of, for example, tally marks, numerals, pictures of models or patterns created, and notes of significant discussions. It is helpful to annotate the samples of work with the date of completion and why it is significant. The records should be updated on a regular basis and used for forward planning. The records will also show areas of experience which the children have not yet had, and aspects which have yet to be assessed. The three record sheets will form the child's record of mathematical achievement and can be passed to the receiving school.

Case studies on assessment

In both these case studies a considerable amount of assessment was undertaken and the outcomes were used for formal planning. The approaches were different, as were the quality of the assessments.

Assessment in a nursery class attached to a primary school

The teacher and nursery nurse kept very careful, detailed records of individual children's progress. From the mathematics focused activity individual children would be assessed. Five children were assessed in detail each week, so that across each half term every child was assessed. Thus, across the year, each child was assessed six times. Also, for any child where there was an observation of significant achievement, this would also be noted. From this targets would be identified for individual children and written notes kept on children's performance on the task set. Each child would be assessed in each curriculum area at least once a term. The teacher and nursery nurse carried out this assessment and, although parent helpers were invited to add their comments, they did not do so. The teacher believed that this was because the parent helpers felt insufficiently confident to make assessments. The assessment documents were open documents and could be accessed by anyone working in the nursery.

Assessment in a nursery school attached to a private preparatory school

The nursery school had recently adopted an assessment book for each child approach to record keeping. These books contained all of the Early Learning Goals, with statements of achievement. Staff added notes on the child's achievement against the goals. The booklets were completed once every three months from the notes that staff kept. Staff noted children's significant achievement on a regular basis, with any of the staff adding to the notes. However, the booklets were kept up-to-date by the manager of the nursery. Every term reports on achievement were sent home to parents and these reports were discussed during the parents' evenings held each term. Similarly, if a child left the nursery to transfer to another one, then a report would be written.

6.5 Partnership with parents and carers

Parental contributions to records

Parents have a wealth of knowledge about their children. When children start nursery it is useful to have a record of what children have already achieved at home, so that appropriate activities, which extend understanding and skills, are planned. Similarly, the evidence of achievement which the nursery builds should be shared with parents so that parents are aware of which aspects of mathematics their child has understood and of areas where they may have difficulty.

Informing parents about mathematics in the nursery

Parents may appreciate information on which aspects of mathematics will be covered during each week. This can be provided through informal discussion, but also through the weekly planning sheet being accessible to parents, perhaps on a notice board. The range of mathematical opportunities which children will have may not be immediately apparent to parents, nor will the importance of building understanding of number. It may be necessary to explain, in a sensitive way, that such young children are not yet ready to 'write sums' and that there is a wealth of mathematics to explore before 'sums' have any meaning for them. Alternative suggestions of activities to try at home will give parents some ideas about appropriate activities for this stage of learning. Parents may appreciate the opportunity to attend a parents' evening at the nursery where they can try some of the activities which their children experience. Where parents agree, some nursery activities can be videoed so that parents can watch videos of their children at work during parents' evenings and be aware of the range of activities which their children have enjoyed. This can encourage parents to ask questions about the purpose of the activities and so extend their knowledge about the range of desirable mathematical experiences which help to build concepts and skills.

Activities to do at home

In Chapters 1 to 5 there are suggestions for encouraging home–nursery links. Often parents or carers will ask how they can help their child at home. The suggestions at the end of each chapter can be used in discussion with parents, or incorporated into leaflets of ideas for home use. In order to encourage this partnership, where there are photographs of the children at work or pictures from the activities or models, these can be displayed in the nursery for others to see. Some nurseries have toy and book libraries run by parents. This can be extended to include mathematical games, toys and books which offer experience in particular mathematical concepts and skills. Parents and carers should be encouraged to use existing domestic routines, such as shopping and cooking, for counting, comparisons of quantities, and for using the language of shape and space, and measures (Aubrey *et al.*, 2000).

Case study of partnership with parents and carers

This case study shows how beneficial home visits can be for the child, the parents and the adults.

A primary school decided to combine their nursery and reception classes to make an early years unit, with ninety children aged from three to five years. Before the children entered the early years unit, a teacher visited them at home, with their parents, and explained the work of the unit to the parents and spent a little time with the child. One teacher commented 'When Mark joined, I had met him, his parents and his brother and sisters. More importantly to Mark, I had met Bert, the black and white dog, and had played with Mark and his toy farm animals. In those first few days at the unit, he would frequently talk to me about Bert. It helped him to settle in and helped us to begin the dialogue with Mark and his parents which will continue whilst he is at this school.'

The school policy was to hold parental and staff discussions about pupils' progress on a termly basis and with the setting up of the unit it was decided to incorporate this into their practice. Parents were asked to come during the evening, as they do in the rest of the school. The child's progress in the nursery was discussed and the parents contributed with their observations from home.

Staff and parents commented on how useful this process was as they were able to share their observations of the child's progress. Staff found that for mathematics learning the meetings had highlighted early on the need to encourage parents to try some mathematical activities at home, as many of the parents regarded mathematics as 'doing sums'. The benefit of this was that a small group of parents offered to set up a toy and book library for the unit and included in the provision were mathematical games, sorting and stacking toys, dominoes and jigsaws, all of which could be borrowed by parents for use at home.

6.6 Professional development in mathematics for nursery staff

So many adults admit to fear and dislike of mathematics. Often this is compounded by the adult's own lack of knowledge and understanding of basic mathematical concepts. The mathematics of the nursery forms the building blocks of children's understanding. Misconceptions, or misuse of language, can inhibit a child's future learning and continue the cycle of mathematically disaffected children who become mathematically disaffected adults. In order to ensure that the adults in the nursery are confident in their mathematical ability, they need to understand the basic concepts and be aware of how these can be developed, both through planned activities and through incidental interactions. In order to encourage such confidence regular staff development sessions which consider mathematical concepts would enhance the adults' own understanding and their awareness of ways in which children learn. This should be built into the planning cycle, so that all have had some opportunity to explore the mathematical opportunities which will be planned for the near future. Adults whose subject knowledge is at least sound help children to learn about mathematics in more effective ways (Menmuir and Adams, 1997). Student teachers, since 1998, have had to undertake further subject knowledge study and satisfy the requirements for subject knowledge within the Standards for Qualified Teacher Status (QTS) (DfEE, 1998). Thus, there is an expectation upon newly qualified teachers, including those working within the Foundation Stage, that their subject knowledge will underpin the learning of children through to the higher ability children in Year 6 and that their subject knowledge is secure so that they teach and guide learning in an encouraging and supportive manner.

It may be appropriate to ask one adult in the nursery to take responsibility for the development of mathematics. This responsibility would include identifying professional development needs and, with the budget holder, finding ways of meeting such needs. Aspects of mathematics which should be considered on a regular cycle for professional development are:

- *Adult confidence with mathematical concepts.* As has been stated before, for many adults, experience of mathematics at school was very unpleasant, and there may well be gaps in mathematical conceptual knowledge and in how children learn.
- *The planning cycle.* A regular review of the nursery's mathematics planning cycle, which covers not just what is included, but how it is explored by the children, will help to identify the strengths and weaknesses of the planning and lead to a more effective approach. Consideration should also be given to the balance of emphasis given to each mathematical topic and whether more or less time is needed for number, for example.
- *Assessment of mathematical concepts and skills.* Reviewing how the assessments are made, what the outcomes of assessments are, how these are recorded, and to what purpose the outcomes are put, will help to ensure that assessment is made for a purpose and that its outcome leads into forward planning. Assessment review will also help to identify any aspects of the mathematics curriculum which are less likely to be assessed on a regular basis, and to identify ways of addressing such issues.
- *Resource provision and organisation.* The range of resources on offer to the children and how these are accessed should be reviewed on a regular basis. This review will offer opportunities to ensure that all adults are familiar with the range of resources and their uses, as well as the learning opportunities that can arise from using specific pieces of equipment.

Glossary

For a fuller account of mathematical terms and their uses, see Holland (1980).

array

objects, or numbers, arranged in rows and columns.

cardinal number

how many there are in a set. The last number in a count is the cardinal value of the set.

classification

identification of an object by specific property/ies, such as colour, texture, shape, or size.

commutativity

the order in which numbers are added makes no difference to the outcome: $3+4=4+3=7$

conservation

of number: recognition that, no matter what order, or how displayed, a given set has the same number of items in it. Young children believe that when the objects are spread out there are more than when they were closer together.

Both sets contain six objects

of length: that two objects of the same length are still the same length when one is moved. Young children believe that the one that is further forward is longer than the other one as they do not compare both ends of the objects.

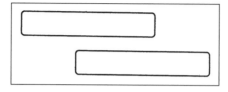

cyclic pattern	arrangement in an enclosed, repeating pattern

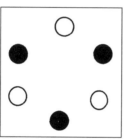

elements	items in a set: for example, in a drawing of a face, the elements would include eyes, ears, nose, and mouth.
enclosure	surrounding, such as the ring drawn for a face.
equivalence	similarity or sameness. *of shape:* two wooden blocks are equivalent when they are the same size and shape. *of number:* having the same numerical value: $3+2=2+3=1+4=5$
iconic recording	recording with marks, such as making tallies.
infinity	where there are no limits of size or number.
linear pattern	a pattern that can be continued to infinity, not closed as in a cyclic pattern.

●○●○●○ ●○

nominal number	a number used to name something: 137 bus number.
order	an arrangement of objects or numbers which shows increases in size or quantity.

ordinal number number used to show an order: coming 2nd in a race; 3rd January; counting the cars, making the red one come third.

partition separate a set into two subsets.

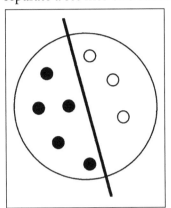

A set of buttons, partitioned by colour, 5 black and 3 white

pattern an arrangement of objects or numbers which follows a rule.

pictograph pictures drawn to represent quantity.

proximity nearby-ness of objects.

schema a repeatable pattern of behaviour which is not tied to specific contexts: examples include making enclosures with bricks; making loops with string; drawing circles.

separation identification of an object from others nearby.

sequence an arrangement of objects. When this is repeated it forms a pattern.

subitise instantly recognise a small quantity, between one and four, without appearing to count how many.

symbolic recording recording with numerals.

tessellation tiling with shapes which fit together leaving no gaps.

A regular tessellation

topology

study of properties of shapes which remain unchanged when they are stretched or bent but not torn. Topology is nicknamed 'rubber geometry' because of the way in which shapes can be transformed by squeezing and stretching one into another.

This triangle made from string has been distorted to another shape

References and Further Reading

Ainley, J. (1991) 'Is there any mathematics in measurement?' In Pimm, D. and Love, E. (eds) *Teaching and Learning School Mathematics*. London: Hodder and Stoughton.

Althouse, R. (1994) *Investigating Mathematics with Young Children*. New York: Teachers College Press.

Askew, M. and Williams, D. (1995) *OFSTED Reviews of Research. Recent Research in Mathematics Education 5–16*. London: HMSO.

Aubrey, A., Godfrey, R. and Godfrey, J. (2000) 'Children's early numeracy experiences in the home', *Primary Practice*, **26**, 36–42.

Aubrey, C. (1993) 'An investigation of the mathematical knowledge and competencies which young children bring into school', *British Educational Research Journal*, **19(1)**, 27–41.

Baroody, A.J. (1987) *Children's Mathematical Thinking*. New York: Teachers College Press.

Baroody, A.J. (2000) 'Does mathematics instruction for three- to five-year-olds really make sense?' *Young Children*, **55(4)**, 61–7.

Bass, H. (1975) 'Topological understanding of young children'. In Rosskopf, M.F. (ed.) *Children's Mathematical Concepts. Six Piagetian Studies in Mathematical Education*. New York: Teachers College Press.

Bergeron, J.C. and Herscovics, N. (1990) 'Kindergartners' knowledge of the preconcepts of number'. In Steffe, L.P. and Wood, T. (eds) *Transforming Children's Mathematics Education. International Perspectives*. Hillsdale, NJ: Lawrence Erlbaum Associates.

Bird, M. (1991) *Mathematics for Young Children: An Active Thinking Approach*. London: Routledge.

Borke, H. (1983) 'Piaget's mountains revisited: changes in the egocentric landscape'. In Donaldson, M. (ed.) *Early Childhood Development and Education*. Oxford: Basil Blackwell.

Bunker, L.K., Johnson, C.E. and Parker, J.E. (1982) *Motivating Kids Through Play*. West Point, NY: Leisure Press.

Caddell, D., Crowther, J., O'Hara, P. and Tett, L. (2000) 'Investigating the roles of parents and schools in children's early years education', paper presented at European Conference on Educational Research, Edinburgh, 20–23 September 2000.

Carraher, T.N. and Schliemann, A.D. (1990) 'Knowledge of the numeration system among pre-schoolers'. In Steffe, L.P. and Wood, T. (eds) *Transforming Children's Mathematics Education. International Perspectives.* Hillsdale, NJ: Lawrence Erlbaum Associates.

Carruthers, E. (1997) 'A number line in the nursery classroom: a vehicle for understanding children's number knowledge', *Early Years,* **18**(1), 9–15.

Charlesworth, R. and Lind, K.K. (1990) *Math and Science for Young Children.* Albany, NY: Delmar.

Choat, E. (1973) *Pre-School and Primary Mathematics.* London: Ward Locke Educational.

Clarke, S. and Atkinson, S. (1996) *Tracking Significant Achievement in Primary Mathematics.* London: Hodder and Stoughton.

Clements, D.H., Swaminathan, S., Hannibal, M.A.Z., and Sarama, J. (1999) 'Young children's concepts of shape', *Journal for Research in Mathematics Education,* **30**(2), 192–212.

Clements, M.A. and Del Campo, G. (1990) 'How natural is fraction knowledge?' In Steffe, L.P. and Wood, T. (eds) (1990) *Transforming Children's Mathematics Education.* Hillsdale, NJ: Lawrence Erlbaum Associates.

Clipson-Boyles, S. (1996) *Supporting Language and Literacy.* London: David Fulton Publishers.

Cohen, D. (1987) *The Development of Play.* London: Routledge.

Copeland, R.W. (1979) *How Children Learn Mathematics. Teaching Implications of Piaget's Research.* New York: Macmillan.

Cox, M.V. and Wright, R. (2000) 'Relative heights of males and females in children's drawings', *International Journal of Early Years Education,* **8**(3), 217–226.

Cubey, P. (1999) 'Exploring Block Play. A study of block play in three early childhood centers in England in January 1998', *Early Childhood Practice,* **1**(1), 6–27.

Davies, M. (1995) *Helping Children to Learn through a Movement Perspective.* London: Hodder and Stoughton.

Department of Education and Science (1988) *Mathematics for Ages 5 to 16. Proposals of the Secretary of State for Education and Science and the Secretary of State for Wales.* London: Central Office of Information.

Department for Education (1995) *Key Stages 1 and 2 of the National Curriculum.* London: HMSO.

Department for Education and Employment (1998) Circular 4/98 'Teaching: high status; high standards. Requirements for courses of initial teacher training'. London: TTA.

Department for Education and Employment (2000) *Curriculum Guidance for the Foundation Stage.* London: QCA.

Dienes, Z.P. (1973) *Mathematics Through the Senses, Games, Dance and Art.* Slough: NFER.

Domoney, B., *et al.* (1991) *Nelson Mathematics: Towards Level 1.* Walton-on-Thames: Nelson.

Dowling, M. (1988) *Education 3 to 5: A Teachers' Handbook.* London: Paul Chapman Publishing.

Early Childhood Mathematics Group (1997) *A Desirable Approach to Learning Mathematics.* Unpublished.

Fuson, K.C., *et al.* (1982) 'The acquisition and elaboration of the number word sequence'. In Brainerd, C.J. (ed.) *Progress in Cognitive Development: Children's Logical and Mathematical Cognition.* New York: Springer-Verlag.

Gardner, K.L., Glenn, J.A. and Renton, A.I.G. (eds) (1973) *Children Using Mathematics. A Report of the Mathematics Section of the Association of Teachers in College and Departments of Education.* Oxford: Oxford University Press.

Geist, E. (2001) 'Children are born mathematicians: promoting the construction of early mathematical concepts in children under five', *Young Children*, 56(4), 12–19.

Gelman, R. (1972a) 'The nature and development of early number concepts'. In Reese, H.W. (ed.) *Advances in Child Development and Behaviour*, vol. 7, pp. 115–67. New York: Academic Press.

Gelman, R. (1972b) 'Logical capacity of very young children: number invariance rules', *Child Development*, **43**, 75–90.

Gelman, R. and Gallistel, C.R. (1986) *The Child's Understanding of Number.* Cambridge, MA: Harvard University Press.

Glenn, J.A. (ed.) (1980) *Children Learn to Measure.* London: Harper and Row.

Groen, G. and Resnick, L.B. (1977) 'Can pre-school children invent addition algorithms?', *Journal of Educational Psychology*, **69**, 645–52.

Gura, P. (ed.) (1992) *Exploring Learning. Young Children and Blockplay.* London: Paul Chapman Publishing.

Haylock, D. and Cockburn, A. (1989) *Understanding Early Years Mathematics.* London: Paul Chapman Publishing.

Hewitt, K. (2001) 'Blocks as a tool for learning: historical and contemporary perspectives', *Young Children*, **56**(1), 6–13.

Hohmann, M., Banet, B. and Weikart, D.P. (1978) *Young Children in Action.* Ypsilanti: The High Scope Press.

Holland, R. (1980) *A Dictionary of Mathematics.* London: Longman.

Hughes, M. (1986) *Children and Number. Difficulties in Learning Mathematics.* Oxford: Basil Blackwell.

Hunting, R.P. and Sharpley, C.F. (1988) 'Fraction knowledge in pre-school children', *Journal for Research in Mathematics Education*, **19**(2), 175–80.

Hutchin, V. (1996) *Tracking Significant Achievement in the Early Years.* London: Hodder and Stoughton.

Lean, G.A. (1988) *Counting Systems of Papua New Guinea.* Lae: Papua New Guinea University of Technology.

Lovell, K. (1971) *The Growth of Understanding in Mathematics: Kindergarten Through Grade Three.* New York: Holt, Rinehart and Winston.

Macnamara, A. (1996). 'From home to school: do children preserve their counting skills?' In Broadhead, P. (ed) *Researching the Early Years Continuum.* Clevedon: Multilingual Matters.

Mason, J. (1991) 'Questions about geometry'. In Pimm, D. and Love, E. (eds) *Teaching and Learning School Mathematics.* London: Hodder and Stoughton.

Matthews, G. and Matthews, J. (1990) *Early Mathematical Experiences.* London: Longman.

Menmuir, J. and Adams, K. (1997) 'Young children's inquiry learning in mathematics', *Early Years,* **17**(2), 34–9.

National Curriculum Council (1989) *Mathematics Non-Statutory Guidance.* York: NCC.

Opie, I. and Opie, P. (eds) (1951) *The Oxford Dictionary of Nursery Rhymes.* Oxford: Oxford University Press.

Patilla, P., Montague-Smith, A. and Broadbent, P. (1995) *Longman Primary Maths. Nursery Handbook.* London: Longman.

Pepper, K.L. and Hunting, R.P. (1998) 'Preschoolers' counting and sharing', *Journal for Research in Mathematics Education,* **29**(2), 164–83.

Piaget, J. (1965) *The Child's Conception of Number.* New York: Norton.

Piaget, J. and Inhelder, B. (1967) *The Child's Conception of Space.* London: Routledge and Kegan Paul.

Piaget, J., Inhelder, B. and Szeminska, A. (1960) *The Child's Conception of Geometry.* London: Routledge and Kegan Paul.

Potter, M.C. and Levy, E.I. (1968) 'Spatial enumeration without counting', *Child Development,* **39**, 265–73.

Pound, L. (1999) *Supporting Mathematical Development in the Early Years.* Buckingham: Open University Press.

Ross, C. and Browne, N. (1993) *Girls as Constructors in the Early Years.* Stoke-on-Trent. Trentham Books.

Scottish Office Education Department (1991) *Curriculum and Assessment in Scotland. National Guidelines Mathematics 5–14.* Edinburgh: HMSO.

Sheridan, M.D. (1977) *Spontaneous Play in Early Childhood.* Windsor: NFER-Nelson.

Stephen, C. and Wilkinson, J.E. (1999) 'Rhetoric and reality in developing language and mathematical skill: plans and playroom experiences', *Early Years,* **19**(2), 62–72.

Thatcher, D. (2001) 'Reading in the math class: selecting and using picture books for math investigations', *Young Children,* **July**, 20–7.

Thompson, I. (1995) 'Pre-number activities and the early years number curriculum', *Mathematics in School,* **24**(1), 37–9.

Thorpe, P. (1995) 'Spatial concepts and young children', *International Journal of Early Years Education*, **3(2)**, 63–73.

Van Oers, B. (1997) 'On the narrative nature of young children's iconic representations: some evidence and implications', *International Journal of Early Years Education*, **5(3)**, 237–45.

Wagner, S. and Walters, J. (1982). 'A longitudinal analysis of early number concepts: from numbers to number'. In Forman, G. (ed.) *Action and Thought*. New York: Academic Press.

Walden, R. and Walkerdine, W. (1982) *Girls and Mathematics: The Early Years*. Bedford Way Papers 8. London: University of London Institute of Education.

Wales, R. (1990) 'Children's pictures'. In Grieve, R. and Hughes, M. (eds) *Understanding Children*. Oxford: Basil Blackwell.

Wheeler, D. (1960) 'The concepts of measurement', *Mathematics Teaching*, **14**.

Womack, D. (1988) *Special Needs in Ordinary Schools. Developing Mathematical and Scientific Thinking in Young Children*. London: Cassell Educational.

Robots

Roamer: Valiant Technology, Myrtle House, 69 Salcott Road, London, SW11 6DQ. Tel: 020 7924 2366

PIP: Swallow Systems, 134 Cock Lane, High Wycombe, Bucks, HP13 7EA. Tel: 01494 813471

Index